BASES
LOADED

What you are about to read has been an extraordinarily difficult experience for me. There is no possible way I could have survived it without the love and support and understanding of my wife. I always tell her that she hit the Lotto on the day she met me, but we both know the truth. And I also want to dedicate this book to my daughter, because everything that her mother and I do is for her.

BASES
LOADED

THE INSIDE STORY *of the* **STEROID ERA**
IN BASEBALL *by the* **CENTRAL FIGURE**
in the **MITCHELL REPORT**

KIRK RADOMSKI

WITH DAVID FISHER

HUDSON
STREET
PRESS

HUDSON STREET PRESS
Published by the Penguin Group
Penguin Group (USA) Inc., 375 Hudson Street, New York, New York 10014, U.S.A.
Penguin Group (Canada), 90 Eglinton Avenue East, Suite 700, Toronto, Ontario, Canada M4P
2Y3 (a division of Pearson Penguin Canada Inc.)
Penguin Books Ltd., 80 Strand, London WC2R 0RL, England
Penguin Ireland, 25 St. Stephen's Green, Dublin 2, Ireland (a division of Penguin Books Ltd.)
Penguin Group (Australia), 250 Camberwell Road, Camberwell, Victoria 3124, Australia (a
division of Pearson Australia Group Pty. Ltd.)
Penguin Books India Pvt. Ltd., 11 Community Centre, Panchsheel Park, New Delhi – 110 017,
India
Penguin Group (NZ), 67 Apollo Drive, Rosedale, North Shore 0632, New Zealand (a division
of Pearson New Zealand Ltd.)
Penguin Books (South Africa) (Pty.) Ltd., 24 Sturdee Avenue, Rosebank, Johannesburg 2196,
South Africa

Penguin Books Ltd., Registered Offices: 80 Strand, London WC2R 0RL, England

First published by Hudson Street Press, a member of Penguin Group (USA) Inc.

First Printing, January 2009
1 3 5 7 9 10 8 6 4 2

Copyright © Kirk Radomski, 2009
All rights reserved

 REGISTERED TRADEMARK—MARCA REGISTRADA
HUDSON
STREET
PRESS
CIP data is available.
978-1-59463-056-9

Printed in the United States of America
Set in Horley Old Style with Foundry Gridnik
Designed by Leonard Telesca

ACKNOWLEDGMENTS

There are so many people whose friendship and support I would like to acknowledge. Among them are those friends I've had for so many years, the people I have depended on, knowing they have my back. These include Steve Cohen, Tommy DePasquale, Anthony Romano, Anthony Marino, Joey Rivera, and my oldest friend Ralph Cosenzo. My friend and my business partner, Vinny Greco, lived through this with me day by day and suffered the media with a smile and only occasionally a nasty word. David Segui is the only ballplayer with the courage to stand up for the truth and I truly thank him for that. I also would like to acknowledge the friendship of Anthony from Doc's Nutrition in Mamaroneck, New York, and my attorney John Reilly and his wonderful secretary, Kathy. The one person who could truly appreciate my situation and remained a close and trusted friend is Brian McNamee, an honest man I'm proud to call my friend. I live on a lovely block in a great neighborhood surrounded by really good people, many of whom were greatly inconvenienced by my actions but never complained and were always supportive. I want them to know that I greatly appreciate them. Of course I want to thank the entire Radomski and

Gaskill families, especially my loving godmother, my aunt Carol. Oddly enough, I also want IRS agent Jeff Novitzky and his entire team to know how much I appreciated their professional attitude at all times; without any exception they were always fair and honest with me.

It's also my pleasure to express my great appreciation to the editor in chief of Hudson Street Press, Luke Dempsey, and the editor I worked with so closely, Meghan Stevenson, for helping me tell this story.

My collaborator, David Fisher, would like to acknowledge the incredibly loving support of his wife, Laura Stevens, and their sons, Jesse and Beau. And also the unbelievably hardworking and extremely competent crew—particularly Suzanne—at the Karmen Executive Center in Seattle, Washington.

BASES
LOADED

ONE

It was June 1994, at Shea Stadium in Queens, New York, and the annual media versus front office game was about to begin. Not that I knew anything about it. I was fast asleep in the Mets locker room, having worked very late the night before, cleaning up the clubhouse after a ball game. And even if I had been awake, I wouldn't have cared. I didn't play baseball and hadn't swung a baseball bat in nearly a decade.

But the Mets beat writers and the front office staff looked forward to this game, so when the media team needed a catcher, Bob Klapisch of the *New York Post* woke me up to ask me to play. "Come on, Bob," I told him, "I'm exhausted. I have to work tonight." But he was persistent. Reluctantly, I agreed. I threw some water on my face, put on my cleats, and went out to the field.

The fact that we were playing at Shea was about all that was professional about the game. I had been working for the Mets for nine years, so I knew just about everybody on the field, but this was the first time I'd played in this game. I came up to bat in the second inning, pulled a Dwight Gooden–model bat out of the bat rack, and took a couple of practice swings. It felt good. Then I walked toward the plate. I knew it was a meaningless game, but I'm a very competitive person. Whatever I do, I push myself to do it as well as possible. I don't like failing at anything.

The pitcher was Drew Marino, a Mets computer analyst and batting-practice pitcher. Drew didn't exactly throw a Doc Gooden fastball. I stepped into the batter's box. Drew went into his windup. I wasn't trying to do anything fancy, just to hit the ball where it was pitched. It was a fastball, about belt high. I swung easily and almost didn't feel the ball hitting the bat.

It just jumped off my bat. In the language of baseball, a home run is called a "long fly." This was a very long fly: a shot to left field that went sailing into the visitors' bullpen. It was about twenty-five feet over the wall. I don't know who was more surprised, me or the other players. But I jogged easily around the bases as if this was something I did every day.

I'm a pretty good athlete but this was completely unexpected. My teammates were thrilled, high-fiving me when I got back to the dugout.

The next time I got up I tried not to get too excited. Once again I swung at a first-pitch fastball. And again the baseball just took off, slamming into the center-field wall almost four hundred feet away. I jogged easily into second base. I forget who was playing shortstop, but he was smiling as he came over to me. "Jesus, Murdoch," he said, calling me by my clubhouse nickname, "how come you're not playing ball somewhere?"

I told him the truth. "Ice hockey's my sport," I said. "Baseball isn't violent enough for me."

I had an unbelievable game: four hits in five or six at bats. In the locker room after the game, everybody was talking about those two long drives. Generally, there aren't any home runs hit in these games. Just reaching the fence once is a big deal. Somebody asked me, "Hey, Murdoch, where'd all that power come from?"

I shrugged my shoulders as if I didn't know. But I knew. Believe me, I knew.

On April 26, 2007, I signed a plea agreement with the U.S. attorney in San Francisco, pleading guilty to one count of distribution of anabolic steroids and one count of money laundering. I definitely was guilty of those two crimes—and a lot more. For more than a decade, I'd been a primary source of illegal steroids and human growth hormones for hundreds of major-league baseball players. My attorney had warned me that I was facing as many as twenty-five years in prison. I had no options; I had admitted being the central figure in what would be called the biggest scandal to hit professional sports since the Chicago "Black Sox" had fixed the 1919 World Series.

I was known throughout baseball as Murdoch, named after hockey star Don Murdoch; I was the guy who could get a player what he needed to excel in the big leagues or to keep him in the game for one more contract, one more season. I was the go-to guy players came to for advice on conditioning and nutrition—and illegal steroids and human growth hormones. I didn't help these players earn millions of dollars; I helped them earn hundreds of millions of dollars. In fact in 2001 I made up a twenty-five-man roster of players I was dealing with and added up their salaries. The total was staggering. My team, the Kirk Radomski team, was earning more than $300 million in salary that season. That was at least $100 million more than the entire Yankees payroll.

I've been called a drug pusher, but I've never thought of myself—or my actions—that way. Many people blame me personally for destroying the integrity of the game. They believe that "juice," as steroids and human growth hormones were commonly known, turned ordinary players into the superstars who broke baseball's most important records. That isn't true. Simply stated, steroids and human growth hormones are not miracle drugs capable of transforming talented athletes into legends.

I certainly wasn't the only person supplying performance-enhancing substances to players. For example, I had absolutely nothing to do with turning Barry Bonds into the man-mountain who smashed Henry Aaron's career home run record. And I had no connection to BALCO, the West Coast laboratory that created tailor-made steroids for professional athletes in several sports. But I was working as a clubhouse attendant for the Mets when the steroid era began in the early 1990s, and by the time it reached its peak a decade later I had become established as the most reliable source in the game. Based on my experience, I can state firmly that what most people think they know about steroids, in fact what they believe they know about all performance-enhancing substances, simply isn't true.

There was absolutely no doubt in my mind that just about everybody in the game, from the clubbies to the team owners, knew that players were using anabolic steroids, human growth hormones, and other substances. It was a secret shared by several thousand people. But because baseball had recovered from the disastrous players' strike in 1994 to become more popular and more profitable than ever before, absolutely nobody wanted to do anything that might hurt the game. The reality is that these substances were easily available to anyone in baseball who wanted to try them. A person who knew what he was doing could walk into a gym pretty much anywhere in America and within a couple of days know what was available and who was selling it, and walk out with as much of it as he could afford. It was even easier to buy these substances in Latin America, where in many countries they were legal and readily available, often sold over the counter in mom-and-pop drug stores.

When in 1986 I led the world champion Mets down Broadway's Canyon of Heroes with the other clubbies, I couldn't have imagined that two decades later I'd be at the center of a huge scandal—and that I would plead guilty to a serious crime. I had started working at Shea when I was fifteen years old, and through the years I made a lot of good friends there. When I fell in love with bodybuilding and became an expert in training, nutrition, supplements, and steroids, it was totally natural that I'd share my knowledge—and my sources—with people I liked and wanted to succeed. If I could help my friends, if I could help my team win, why wouldn't I?

When I began answering questions from players about steroids, and eventually supplying them with whatever they needed, it never occurred to me that it could lead to a prison sentence. Baseball has a long tradition of ignoring cheating—from pitchers throwing spitballs to teams using television cameras to steal signs—until someone finally gets caught and makes it impossible to ignore. When I started in baseball, the official drug policy seemed to be "don't get caught." But when Congress held hearings in 2005 to investigate the use of performance-enhancing substances, and baseball basically told them to butt out, I began to suspect that it might be time to find a good criminal lawyer.

My life as a felon began at 6:00 a.m. on December 15, 2005. A few minutes earlier I'd heard several cars pulling up and stopping in front of my house on Long Island. I heard car doors opening and closing. When I looked out the window, I saw two vans and probably six unmarked cars lined up neatly. Well, I thought, this definitely ain't good.

I told my wife to get up. She had absolutely no idea what I had been doing—none. But it was pretty obvious that she was about to find out. I watched as a tall, bald man walked purposefully up the front walk. From photographs I'd seen in newspapers and magazines, I was pretty sure it was Jeff Novitzky, the IRS agent leading the investigation into steroid and growth hormone use in professional sports.

I raced downstairs, even though I was still dressed in my underwear. I wanted to open the door before Novitzky could ring the bell and wake up my daughter. When I opened it, I was looking directly at Novitzky. He identified himself and then held up a piece of paper. "I've got a search warrant for your home."

"Let me see it," I said. I knew that if a search warrant didn't have a seal, it had not been signed by a judge and was invalid. If this one wasn't sealed, I wouldn't have to let them inside. Unfortunately, the warrant had a seal.

He asked evenly, "Do you know why I'm here?"

Of course I knew why he was standing on my front step. My whole life had led to this morning. But surprisingly, I was calm, as if somewhere in my mind I'd been preparing for this moment for a long time. "Yeah, I got a pretty good idea," I told him. "Are you gonna arrest me?" If they planned to arrest me I wanted it done before my daughter got up. The last thing I wanted her to see was her father being taken away in handcuffs. "I've got my wife and my daughter here. My daughter needs to go to school in an hour."

"We'd like to do this quietly," he replied. As he spoke I glanced over his shoulder. To me it looked like a small army of neatly dressed agents was standing out there by their cars, just watching and waiting for directions. Novitzky began telling me how much he already knew about my life, from the way I earned a living to the fact that my neighbor was a cop. Obviously they had done their homework. They knew everything.

"Listen, I got to talk to my lawyer," I told him. I was bluffing. I didn't even know a criminal lawyer. "So if you are going to arrest me, let's go now. I'll call him later."

Novitzky surprised me. "No no no," he said, shaking his head. "We're not here to arrest you. We just need to talk to you."

Oh, that was interesting. Suddenly I understood: they wanted information from me. Maybe they didn't know as much as I suspected. Maybe I wasn't looking at my own doom. They *need* to talk to me. It was as if someone had suddenly tossed me a lifeline.

Novitzky continued, "Have you got any anabolics or growth hormones in the house right now?"

They had a valid search warrant. There was nothing I could do to keep them from searching the house. "Yeah," I admitted, "I've got a few things here." I swung open the door and invited them into my home.

TWO

So I—the guy who led the Mets' 1986 victory parade down Broadway, just a clubhouse attendant but very much part of an extraordinary team—stood aside and let Jeff Novitzky's investigators into my home. I had never been more alone.

Growing up, baseball had never been my passion. I wasn't much of a baseball fan. Although I grew up a few miles from Yankee Stadium, I was not one of those kids who lived and died with the Yankees. I knew a lot about baseball, but I was too busy living my own life to become emotionally involved. I certainly didn't care at all about the Mets, who were playing their games at Shea Stadium in Flushing, Queens. To me the Mets could have been on the other side of the world rather than just on the other side of the city.

But then I was given an opportunity that many teenagers would cut off their arm to get: Charlie Samuels, who was then and is now the Mets' equipment manager, rented the basement apartment in my friend's house, just around the block. Charlie has always been a friend, a man I could trust. When he needed some help at Shea, he asked my friend to work for him, and eventually he hired everybody in the neighborhood. In 1985 I went to work part time in the visiting-team clubhouse.

I know that being paid to work in a major-league clubhouse would be a dream come true for a lot of people, but for me it was little more than a good job. While the money was decent—we were paid a small salary by the Nelson Doubleday–owned Mets but earned most of our money from tips—the job consisted of numerous not-so-glamorous duties like picking up underwear, washing bundles of sweaty uniforms, cleaning out lockers, scraping mud out of cleats and shining them, and running countless errands of every kind for the players.

The best part of the job, which I grew to really enjoy, was getting to know the players as real people. While working in the visiting-team clubhouse, I got to meet great stars like Pete Rose, Dave Parker, Dale Murphy, Mad Dog Madlock, and Gary Carter (who was then with the Expos). Over time we learned what each player wanted waiting for him in the clubhouse when he got to New York, from cases of Gatorade to the big bucket of Yoo-hoo we would have ready for Lee Mazzilli.

While working there, I learned the only rules that mattered to clubbies: do whatever the players, managers, and coaches ask you to do. And keep your mouth shut about everything you do, you see, and you hear. Whatever happens in the clubhouse is private. The first time you talk about it might well be the last time. The Mets can—and will—replace you in a second. There was no flexibility in that rule. From the first day I walked through those double doors, I was taught that by being there we were part of a very special, extremely exclusive, tight-knit club. And if I talked about it, I wasn't going to be there for very long.

During my first month on the job, the Mets were playing their National League East rivals, the Philadelphia Phillies, at Shea Stadium. For some reason, truthfully I don't remember, I was told to put on a Phillies uniform and work the game as a ball boy. That meant I had to sit on a stool down the third-base line and catch foul ground balls that came down the line. The most important part of the job was remembering that if a playable foul pop-up came toward me, I had to pick up my stool and get out of the players' way. Even though I claimed not to be a big baseball fan, I have to admit it was exciting: I was fifteen years old and I was sitting on a major-league field during a game in New York City, wearing a real major-league uniform. A year earlier I'd had to pay my way into a ballpark, suddenly I was on the field. Like so many other things I did at Shea, this reinforced the feeling that this opportunity was something very special.

The glamour and excitement lasted about half an inning—just until some serious Met fans objected pretty loudly to the hated Phillies uniform I was wearing—and began throwing beer on me. At the end of that inning, I ran into the clubhouse and changed into the flashy orange and blue Mets uniform.

As clubbies, my friends and I did whatever we were asked to do, even if sometimes it seemed questionable. Early in the 1985 season, the Pittsburgh Pirates came to town for a three-game series. That was the first time I met Pirates manager Chuck Tanner. He sent me to a nearby off-track betting parlor to place bets for him, and then to go back later and collect his winnings. I was too young to be betting legally, but no one ever objected. In fact I was too young to drive, so I had to recruit an older clubbie to take me over there and back. It didn't even occur to me that it was illegal. But even if I'd realized it, I would have done it anyway. The job was saying yes to every request. I placed bets because Chuck Tanner, who was a terrific guy, asked me to place bets. And I never whispered a word about it to anyone outside those double doors.

Eventually, I worked as a Mets batboy, and I learned pretty quickly that there were secrets out on the field too. One of our stars sometimes used a corked bat. That meant that the barrel of the bat had been drilled out, cork had been put inside it, and it had been resealed. Supposedly, this caused the ball to travel a lot farther. Corking a bat is definitely against the major-league rules, but it had been going on long before I got there. This player didn't use a corked bat all the time, just in key situations. Eventually, rumors spread around the league that he was using a loaded bat, and one night after a game in Houston someone from the Astros organization broke into our bat bag and stole one of his bats, presumably to x-ray it. The corked bats had colored dots on the bottom of the handles, so we knew that the Astros had taken one of them. We had to assume that they'd checked the bat and confirmed that it was corked. As batboys, we knew exactly what we had to do to prevent Houston from getting this player suspended. The league couldn't prove that he used a corked bat unless it was confiscated by an umpire after being used in a game.

My job as the batboy was to get the bat as soon as the player hit the ball, before Houston could protest and the umpire picked it up. Get that bat, no matter what. Each time this player came to bat, I was poised on the top step of the dugout, ready to move. Late in one game he hit a long shot to right. I was racing out of that dugout before the bat even hit the ground. I picked it up, quickly turned around, and started jogging back to the dugout. Behind me, I could hear the umpire start yelling, "Hey! You! Gimme that bat. Gimme that bat." I didn't even hesitate—I just kept going. The umpire started chasing after me.

Just as I reached the top step of the dugout, I made a big show of tripping, and, naturally, as I did I dropped the bat, which went thunking down the dugout steps. While lying there, I grabbed the clean bat that we'd left on the top step in preparation for this exact situation. I got to my feet and handed the replacement bat to the umpire. Naturally, when it was sent to the commissioner's office and x-rayed, it was found to be absolutely normal.

In the sense of forging relationships, being in the dugout during a major-league game is almost like going into battle. While I did make some strong friendships, the truth is that I didn't particularly like working as a batboy. Baseball bored me. Occasionally, in fact, I got so bored that I would fall asleep. The Mets manager at the time, Davey Johnson, actually had to tell Charlie Samuels to "make sure your batboys get some sleep at night so they don't fall asleep in the dugout."

As a kid I had assumed that the dugout was a lively, noisy place during a game, with players cheering for their teammates. I suppose I got that idea from sandlot and Little League games. It's possible that it's changed since I got out of baseball, but when I was there, the dugout was quiet and intense. The players were focused totally on the game. The only time you'd hear a player was when he was shouting encouragement to a batter or pitcher. Otherwise they were totally focused on the moment, unbelievably zoned in.

There were no distractions, and conversation was limited. I never said a word unless I was asked a direct question. Off the field many of these players were my friends, people I'd partied with the night before, but the field was their office and when we were there it was all business. Wally Backman, for example, was definitely our most intense player—it was as if he was in a different world during a game—but I couldn't talk to Ray Knight or Keith Hernandez either. Lenny Dykstra was a rookie during my first year with the organization, and he learned from Backman and doubled his intensity level. There was no joking in the dugout, no playing around: the only thing that mattered was the game.

The players were constantly moving around during the game. Often before a player came to bat, he'd go to the batting cage under the stands to get loose, or up the ramp into the clubhouse to watch the game on television and try to see what the opposing pitcher was throwing. The Mets videotaped every at bat, and sometimes players would watch tapes of their last at bat against a particular pitcher to see what pitches he'd thrown and how he'd located them. On the major-league level, hitting or pitching isn't sport: it's almost science—with millions of dollars at stake. And on that level, the difference between most players' talent isn't very wide—so what matters is how they translate their talent into performance. The players were always looking for an edge, any edge, because even the slightest advantage could make a huge difference in one at bat, in a single game, in the whole season or their entire career.

I worked for the Mets organization for a decade. Officially, the clubbies' job consisted of making sure the uniforms were clean when the players arrived and then washed after the game. We shined their cleats and packed their bags before road trips. We marked their bats and put them in the bat rack. We cleaned the lounge, the manager's office, and the bathrooms. We made sure the catered food arrived hot and on time. We filled the resin bags for the coming season in the winter, unlocked the doors for spring training, and at the end of the season packed up players' homes. We made sure the players' free passes went to the right people. We solved whatever problems came up, and we imitated the players' signatures on baseballs and memorabilia so they wouldn't have to spend time doing it. Like other clubbies, I signed countless balls and photographs; I got so good at it that I could forge the signatures of Mets players almost as well as the players could sign them themselves.

Unofficially, we did everything else. Like so much in life, baseball players are better seen at a distance. The Mets were just like any other team—the players were idolized by the fans, but on a daily basis they were no different from other people, except that they were being paid millions of dollars and had women constantly available to them. Any teenage illusions I might have had that major leaguers were special lasted only as long as it took me to get to know them. Some were among the best human beings I've been fortunate to know, while a few others were real assholes. And some of what went on behind the double doors would really surprise fans.

I remember the women that hung around: two girls we called the Titty Sisters, for example, and other girls who serviced players in the bullpen during games. Once I had to hide in the trainer's room because someone was outside trying to serve a subpoena forcing me to testify in a paternity suit being brought against a player by a former girlfriend. Another time I testified for the Mets in a case in which a groupie, who'd made herself available to the team, claimed that a player had threatened to kill her for antagonizing another player's wife.

I also saw the occasional fight inside the clubhouse. One night after a game, a player made racial remarks to a teammate. The second player blew up and went after him. It was almost like a bar brawl in an old western: they crashed into tables and sent food flying all over the locker room. The truth is that the first player didn't mean what he said and apologized the next day. By the start of the game these players were friends and teammates again. Everybody inside the clubhouse knew about it, including the sportswriters, but nobody outside ever found out about it.

As part of my job, I got to see players at the most vulnerable and exciting moments of their lives. I would drive over to LaGuardia Airport to pick up minor leaguers who had just been called up to the big leagues, and on occasion I would drive a player to the airport after he had been traded or released. Believe me, there are few silences more painful than driving somewhere with a player who is traveling to the end of his dream. I drove guys to the hospital when their children were born. I was invited to baptisms and weddings and every kind of personal event.

The clubbies were the best source of information about the team. Generally, we knew about the decisions being made concerning a player's future long before the player did, particularly during spring training. Every spring in Port St. Lucie, Florida, we'd watch young players fighting to make the team and veterans struggling to hold on for one final season. Both the kids and the veterans would beg us for information:

16

"You hear anything?"

"Am I going north with the ball club?"

"What do you think?"

We always claimed that we didn't know, but because it was our job to pack the uniforms, we were in fact usually the first people to know who was going to New York. I never told a player what I knew, just in case the front office changed its mind; the last thing I wanted was to either get a player's hopes up or crushed—and then be wrong.

There was very little to do in Port St. Lucie. The players and clubbies spent all day, every day, at the ballpark, but at night we'd go to dinner or to the movies or to whatever we were going to do as a group. We played a lot of miniature golf, for example—so much that I probably can still putt a golf ball through the spinning sails of a windmill and into a clown's laughing mouth. We'd hold tournaments and play for dinner the next night—even though when the clubbies lost the players never made us pay. Video games were just starting to get popular, and in particular the players loved the video baseball games. These were early generation games, before the graphics got good, and they used the names and images of real players. Bobby Bonilla even had a box made for the game and the monitor that he carried around all season. We set up a video game system in the clubbies' rented house, and the players would come by and bring food. We'd stay up all night playing.

Pitcher Roger McDowell lived near the ballpark and each year he'd have a barbecue for the clubbies. After reliever John Franco's wife left to take their kids back to school we'd hang out with him almost every night. In those days everyone who worked for the organization was treated like a member of a big family.

The friendships we made in Florida continued in New York. It was a wonderful clubhouse, with lots of energy. McDowell was the practical joker who kept everybody loose. He was our acknowledged master of the hotfoot—the fine art of using matches to literally set fire to the foot of a person not paying attention. If anybody closed their eyes for two minutes, even in the dugout, Roger would attack. He would put bubble gum in his teammates' hair, and when the team was in a batting slump, it was Roger who would throw firecrackers at the bat rack to "wake up the bats." Although sometimes we were the butt of the jokes, the other clubbies and I were included in everything that took place.

There was always something going in the clubhouse. I remember, for example, the time *Tonight Show* host Jay Leno came in to say hello and one of the players began telling him about the famed "three man lift." This is an unbelievable feat of strength and science in which three large men lie down on the floor and are tied together with belts. Then the smallest man on the team takes hold of the belt and literally lifts them several inches off the floor. The Mets, it was explained to Leno, played the three man lift as a betting game, with money being wagered on whether a particular player could pick up the three men. Leno didn't believe it was possible, so it was decided to show him. Some money was bet—and then someone suggested that Leno be the man in the middle. He was a big guy, it was pointed out, so he'd make it even harder to lift the trio. He would certainly win the bet. Leno agreed and lay down on the clubhouse floor. He was tied tightly with belts and some cord I found in the trainer's room. And once he was unable to move, the players came out of their stalls carrying whatever crap they could find and threw it at him. Of course nobody could pick up three people by a belt! But he'd been warned—we told him it was an unbelievable feat.

We also successfully employed the moose horn. The moose horn was a U-shaped horn with valves, but the valves had all been stuffed. Well, not exactly all of them. The one that wasn't stuffed was aimed directly at the person blowing the horn. We would pack it with powder and tell a rookie that "It's time to call the moose! You have to blow really hard or the horn doesn't work." And the rookie, wanting to be liked, would blow into that horn with all his strength—and blow that wad of powder right into own face.

We would do almost anything for a laugh. Shoelaces were knotted together, and Icy Hot Balm or Atomic Balm was loaded into jockstraps. Randy Myers loved to wrestle the batboys. To prove how strong he was he'd try to pick them up and body slam them. Sometimes, long after a night game ended, we'd clear out the center of the clubhouse to create a ring and hold mock wrestling championships. The Mets clubhouse was filled with a lot of big kids having fun.

And I can't describe some of the X-rated practical jokes that took place behind the clubhouse doors. Way behind the clubhouse doors. But those jokes, which even now can't be shared with anyone outside the team, really helped strengthen our bonds.

Because we worked together and played together, I'd get to know even more about a player's life than members of his own family. I applied for their first credit cards; I wrote checks for them and paid their bills; I even went to the bank and withdrew cash from their accounts when they needed it. Surprisingly, we had young players earning more than a million dollars a year who had never written a check.

Some of these tasks impacted my own life. I bought plane tickets for several ballplayers' girlfriends with my mother's credit cards so their wives wouldn't find out. Actually, one of my jobs was keeping girlfriends and wives apart. One player, for instance, had his girlfriend staying in his apartment after his wife went back to their off-season home. But one day his wife unexpectedly returned and decided to come to a home game. His girlfriend was furious that his wife was back—so she showed up at the same game wearing an outfit she'd borrowed from the wife's closet. The player glanced into the stands from the dugout and was stunned, absolutely stunned, when he saw his girlfriend wearing his wife's clothes and moving toward the family section. This was a disaster about to happen.

"Kirk!" he screamed to me. "I don't care what you have to do, but you gotta stop her. She's wearing my wife's dress!" I raced into the stands to try to head off a crisis. With the assistance of the ushers—who were also friends of all the clubbies—I managed to keep the player's girlfriend far away from the family section where his wife was sitting.

It seemed like there was always some sort of unusual problem we had to figure out how to deal with. Once, while cleaning out a single player's locker we discovered that he had contracted genital crabs. Obviously he was embarrassed, so he hadn't told anyone about it. But because crabs are highly contagious and a locker room is the ideal breeding place for that type of thing, we had to wash his clothes separately and clean out every locker near his. Imagine what would have happened if a faithful married player contracted crabs while playing for the Mets? Is there a wife in the world who would believe that he was completely innocent?

So I'm not exaggerating when I explain that when I worked for the Mets between 1985 and 1995 players trusted clubbies with every aspect of their lives. Even when the team went on the road and we stayed home, they would sometimes leave their cars with us, to use or have some work done on them. It was always, "Get me some new tires," or "You know somebody who can fix that dent?" or "It needs the regular check-up."

Whatever needed to be done on a car, a clubbie would make sure it got done. With all the friends I have in that business up in the Bronx, it was not hard. Admittedly, there were some benefits in it for us too. Lenny Dykstra had a beautiful yellow Mitsubishi, for example, that he would let me use when the team was on the road. You think it didn't feel unbelievable to pull up in front of my high school in a bright yellow thirty-thousand-dollar sports car?

A lot of the things we were asked to do were pretty boring. If a player forgot something at home, a clubbie would drive there and bring it back. If a player needed someone to wait in his apartment for the cable guy or the phone company, a clubbie would do it for him. Once several of us spent an afternoon at Darryl Strawberry's house, although I don't remember what we were doing there. We decided to make coffee. Fortunately, there was a container of milk in the refrigerator and we used it. Unfortunately, we'd forgotten that Darryl's wife was breast-feeding at the time and . . . and . . . I will never forget the look on Straw's face as he told us, "You guys drank all my wife's breast milk."

"I'm begging you," I said to him. "Don't tell me that."

Being a clubbie was a year-round job. After a while I was doing it as much for the friendships I formed as for the money, though the money helped. I was brought up with a very strong work ethic: no matter what the job was, you broke your ass to get it done and get it done right. So whatever it took to earn a legal living, I was willing to do it.

The Mets paid by the hour, but a lot of the money we earned consisted of tips from the players. As I got older and started working pretty much full time, I earned about thirty-five thousand dollars a year in salary and tips. Most players would tip you for each of the errands you did for them. After batting practice, for example, eight players might each hand me twenty dollars, asking me to run upstairs for hot dogs and telling me to keep the change. On a real good trip I could earn as much as a hundred dollars. At the end of the season, each player on the roster would give each clubhouse attendant a lump sum. If the team made the playoffs, the players always would vote to give the clubhouse workers a playoff share to split, which could be a substantial amount of money. Believe it or not, when players earned less money they tipped the clubhouse attendants better. In the early 1980s, when a million dollars was still a great salary, at the end of the season each player would tip me five hundred or a thousand dollars. But when salaries went up, tips went down; because, I think, with the higher salaries came a sense of entitlement.

The big salaries seemed to change the attitude in the clubhouse. When I was there, the younger players used to be taken under the tutelage of the older players, who would explain how baseball worked. When Doc Gooden and Straw came up, for example, the veterans taught them how to dress properly, where to buy good suits at better prices, and how to conduct themselves off the field as major leaguers. That included how to tip the clubhouse guys. The veterans taught the younger players what to tip the main guys, the part-timers, and the kids who ran the errands.

A lot of the veteran players were very generous. The biggest tip I ever received was from David Cone. I was buying my first brand-new car, but to pay for it I had to sell my old car. I was in the clubhouse when I got a call from the dealer in Pennsylvania telling me my new car was in. I told him, "I need a week or two until I can get rid of my other car."

Coney was sitting there watching TV and overheard the conversation. When I got off the phone he handed me a blank check and said, "Fill it in for whatever you need."

I couldn't believe it. I told him no, that wasn't necessary.

He insisted. "Just get your car. Don't worry about it. When you sell your car, take care of it."

I filled in the blank check for five thousand dollars. After I'd sold my car, I tried to give the money back to him but he refused to take it. "Just get out of here," he said. "That's not even a day's pay—just don't worry about it."

The man wouldn't take his money back. So I said, "You know what, don't give me any more money this year." At the end of the year I refused to take any money from him—so he left my end-of-the-season tip in my bag.

As I've said, I wasn't a huge baseball fan, and I didn't work in the clubhouse for the prestige or the status. Outside the locker room, attendants like me were just anonymous people who the fans pushed out of the way or, worse, tried to use to get closer to the players or to get an autograph or a piece of used equipment. After I graduated from high school I could have taken many different jobs, but I continued working for the Mets because I enjoyed the people and treasured the friendships I'd made, relationships that in many cases continued long after I'd quit my job—or at least until the IRS showed up at my front door. After all, I was in the clubhouse when Dwight Gooden, Darryl Strawberry, Sid Fernandez, Coney, and Howard Johnson became stars; I was there when veterans like Gary Carter, Rusty Staub, and Keith Hernandez formed the heart of the team.

I became particularly close to younger players like Doc and Straw. Nike often would give them clothes and equipment, which they would pass along to us. Doc used to take all the clubbies out for dinner at Benihana and would never let anyone else pick up the check. What I remember most about Doc and Straw is that they would come up to my neighborhood in the Bronx and play Wiffle ball and basketball with the kids there. In the past, newspapers had always made a big deal of the fact that in his prime Willie Mays would play stickball with kids in the street. For a time Doc and Straw were just as big in New York as Willie, and still they would come up to the Bronx to play Wiffle ball with the neighborhood kids on Barnes Avenue. Even after Doc won the Cy Young Award as the best pitcher in baseball, he came to the Bronx. If we weren't playing Wiffle ball, I'd get the keys to my old grammar school, Our Lady of Solace, and we'd spend the afternoon playing basketball with the local kids.

My friendships extended beyond the Mets players. Baseball is really a close-knit fraternity, and if you earned your membership, players from other teams trusted you as much as your own people did. When I worked in the visiting-team clubhouse, I started a lot of good relationships. I met Pete Rose, for example, and later became close friends with his son. More than most players, Pete understood and honored his obligations as a major leaguer. There are players who willingly sign things for fans. Gary Carter was just great for that, for example. No one was better at signing autographs than Pete. Even though he barely knew me, I could bring him twenty things to sign and he'd sign every one of them without a complaint. When a fan asked him for something, he tried to do it. He knew what his responsibility was.

When word got around that during the winter some friends and I rented ice time in the middle of the night to play hockey, several players told me they wanted to get in the game. Craig Biggio lived in New Jersey, and he'd drive more than two hours to play, even though we didn't get on the ice until one o'clock in the morning. Lee Mazzilli, who was a championship speed skater, used to play with us. Both Bobby Bonilla and his brother Javier learned how to skate so they could play. With people like this there was never any status bullshit. There was no difference between players and clubhouse guys. We hit them hard and they tried to hit us back harder. Although for a long time Bobby Bonilla was just happy to be able to stand up on skates.

We were friends, in other words, who hung out, played games, and then got something to eat. And later, when these same guys started asking me questions about fitness or if I could get some juice or supplements or, later on, growth hormones for them, I thought of it as simply doing a favor for a friend. I wasn't supplying drugs; I was helping people get back to work, perform at the peak of their abilities, or prolong their careers. The mentality was exactly the same as it had been when I was working in the clubhouse.

It was the 1986 season that really bonded us together as a team forever. I was there for most of the magic moments on the very improbable road to the world championship. I was only sixteen years old, and every moment of that season is going to live in my memory forever. At least for me, that team would always be the real Miracle Mets.

I was sitting on the top step of the Mets dugout during the sixth game when Red Sox first baseman Bill Buckner committed what might be the most infamous error in baseball history. The Boston Red Sox, up 5–3, were one out away from breaking baseball's most well-known curse and winning their first championship since 1918. All season long the Mets had been able to find miraculous ways to win, but it looked like our incredible streak had run out. For me it had been a very rough week because my uncle had died. I didn't want to go home and have to deal with the grief, so I'd slept in the clubhouse for the past three nights. At the start of the bottom of the tenth inning the dugout was completely dead. Then, with two outs, the Mets started a comeback that probably ranks second in baseball history only to Bobby Thomson's 1951 National League pennant–winning home run. But this was for the world championship.

With two outs, Gary Carter and Kevin Mitchell singled. Believe me, not one person in that dugout was giving up, but scoring two runs with two outs didn't seem very likely. Ray Knight got two strikes on him, so the Red Sox were only one strike away from the championship. One strike, one pitch, it would make all the difference in so many lives. Knight singled to make the score 5–4. The next batter, Mookie Wilson, also got two strikes and then kept fouling off pitch after pitch. In the dugout we were dying and praying with each pitch. Then Red Sox pitcher Bob Stanley threw a wild pitch, which allowed Mitchell to score the tying run. I was sixteen years old and I was in baseball heaven. These weren't the Mets: they were my friends.

Then Mookie hit a routine ground ball to first baseman Bill Buckner. Most major leaguers, but especially a great fielder like Buckner, would make it 999-plus times out of 1,000. We're going to extra innings, I figured, but we're alive, we're back in the game. I was sitting in the dugout, right next to the camera box, no more than fifty feet from Buckner. There is a photograph of me sitting there with my mouth wide open, watching as the ball rolled through Buckner's legs. We were all silent for a split second because no one in our dugout, no one in the stadium, could believe it. Bill Buckner would never miss that ball. When it happened I thought, "Jesus, someone is on our side today."

Compared to the classic sixth, the seventh game was anticlimactic. Even though we were down three runs, no one had any doubt that we were going to come back to win it. When we went ahead, my boss, Charlie Samuels, came over to me in the dugout and warned me that after the last out was made fans were going to come pouring out of the stands, and they would be grabbing anything they could find. The dugout was going to be protected by cops, but the players were going to be on the field. My job, he said, was to "Make sure no equipment gets taken. Nobody gets nothing."

At the end of the game everything happened just like he said it would. When the final out was made, everybody came tearing out of the dugout, sprinting across the first base line to leap onto the pile in the middle of the field. I ran out there with everybody else. A classic photograph of that moment appeared on the cover of the *Sporting News*, and there I was, right in the middle of the celebration. Everyone was leaping and laughing; it was a moment of unbelievable joy.

Seconds after we raced onto the field, it seemed like half of the people in the ballpark came out of the stands to join us. It was magical—our fans were celebrating right alongside the players. But then I saw a kid in a blue shirt grabbing Gary Carter's helmet. Suddenly, I remembered Charlie's warning, "Nobody gets nothing." I practically tackled that kid. I threw my arm around his neck and brought him down. I grabbed the helmet and the police descended on him. I had done my job.

We stayed in the locker room, partying almost all night; back then the Mets were an organization that wanted to celebrate together. But when the party ended in the early hours of the morning, and the players left to get ready for the parade, it was our job to clean up the place. It was a total mess, the only time I've ever seen a carpet soaked with champagne. By the time we got finished, there was just enough time to get ready for the parade.

To march in the parade, the clubbies were required to wear Mets uniforms. I think I wore Lenny Dykstra's pants. I don't remember whose jersey I borrowed. Each of the players rode in a convertible or on a float. The batboys and the clubhouse personnel got to lead the parade, carrying the world championship banner. We walked down Broadway in a shower of confetti. We'd been told to make sure we wore glasses so we wouldn't get hit in the eye with something thrown from a high window, like one of the giant floppy disks people used in the 1980s. Fortunately, even with more than a million people cheering, there were no problems. It remains the loudest roar I've ever heard, which is pretty loud considering I'd also heard the sellout crowd at Shea during the playoffs.

Just two years later, the Mets were heavily favored to win another world championship. There was no question that we had the best team that year, but we lost the league championship playoffs to the Los Angeles Dodgers. That flight home from California was the longest trip of my life, maybe even longer than the flight to San Francisco to make my guilty plea. No one in the organization believed we could lose. We were the Miracle Mets, fate didn't let us lose. On the bus going to the airport not a single person said a word. I remember we got caught in a traffic jam because there had been a fatal car accident. We had a police escort, so they waved us right past the wrecked cars. It was an awful scene, and the police lights made it look even more bizarre. But somehow the devastation of that accident seemed fitting given what had just happened to us on the field. As exhilarated as we had been two years earlier, that's how depressed we all were that night.

By the early 1990s, I was about the same age as the young players coming up from the minors, so after games a group of us would often go out together somewhere. Since I knew my way around the city, players were always asking me, "Where you going tonight? What are you going to do?" There were always a few players who would hang out in the clubhouse for several hours after the game, waiting for the attendants to finish work so we could all go out together. Todd Hundley, David Segui, Doc, and Straw were among those who'd wait. We'd go to restaurants up in the Bronx for the best Italian food in New York. When we went to clubs, I made sure I knew the bouncers so they would watch my back and see that the players had no problems. Some of the guys were from rural areas and had no concept of the rules of a street fight; the rules being there are no rules. So when we were in a bar, I made sure that no drunken asshole trying to earn a reputation by punching out a Met took a swing at one of my guys. In my life, my friends come first. If I'm out with someone, I'm going to make sure they get home safely. By that point I'd been training for several years and was pretty big, so when I stepped in the middle people showed me respect and backed off. Players liked going out with me because I knew where to go; I didn't drink, so I was the permanent designated driver; and if there were problems, the players knew I would take care of them.

Strip clubs were just starting to become popular around this time, and sometimes we'd end up going to one of them and staying there the whole night and into the following morning; then we'd go right back to the stadium in time for the game. A few of the players loved gambling in Atlantic City, so on occasion we'd climb into a limo after a game and come back the next afternoon. We were in New York City: there was always something going on, always someplace to go.

In July of 1988, for example, I often went out with Dwight Gooden and we got to be good friends. At that time baseball was having problems with players using recreational drugs like marijuana and cocaine, and not yet with performance-enhancing drugs. The fear was that players would get involved with drug dealers and do things to affect the integrity of the game, and also that players would become addicted. It was potentially a very serious problem. Gooden had tested positive for drugs, and under the drug treatment program then in existence, his urine was being tested regularly to make sure he had stopped.

We used to break his chops about it. "Hey, Doc, the pee guy's here!" We all thought that was a pretty strange job. We could just imagine this guy answering questions about what he did for a living. I'll bet he told people he worked for major-league baseball. "Doing what?"

"Going around watching guys pee." It was pretty funny until the day it got serious.

"I gotta talk to you," Doc said. I could see he was shaken. "The pee guy's here and I can't pee. I went out with a couple of guys the other night, and if he tests me I'm gonna get suspended."

He didn't tell me if he had used marijuana or cocaine. But it didn't matter. Under the rules of baseball, if he tested positive he was going to be suspended without pay. He was earning $2.2 million, which meant that a suspension could have cost him as much as a million dollars. He wasn't as concerned about that as he was about letting down his teammates. Doc never wanted to disappoint anyone.

"What do you want me to do?" Everybody knew I didn't do drugs. They'd seen me turn them down.

"Will you pee for me?" he asked.

Maybe it sounds humorous, but it wasn't. My friend was in a jam, so of course I was going to help him. I told him I'd do it. I don't remember how I learned all the details of the testing program, but I knew that they measured the temperature of the urine sample just after it was collected to make sure it was fresh and came from the person being tested. They split the sample into two batches and registered the temperature. Both samples had to be right around body temperature.

I had never done anything like this before. Fortunately, someone in the clubhouse had just had a baby and was handing out cigars in long metal tins. I grabbed one of them and told Doc, "I'll piss into this thing and heat it up. You wait about five minutes, let it cool down. Once it starts to feel like body temperature put it in your pants and go into the men's room. Walk right in there but don't go right away. Wait a couple of minutes. I'll be in the doctor's office. When you hear me make some kind of noise to distract him, just pour it into his cup." Of all the odd things I've done for friends in my lifetime, peeing into a cigar tin might be the strangest. But I did it and handed it to Doc. Our plan worked perfectly. Doc passed his pee test.

About three weeks later the pee guy showed up in the clubhouse again. Once more Doc came to me. "I'm not sure if it's out of my system. I'm afraid." I thought about it a lot harder this time.

I would have done anything for Doc. But this made me uncomfortable. I'd seen drugs destroy the lives of people I cared about. I took it very seriously. "Okay, Doc, I'll do it one more time," I told him. "But if you're doing drugs you've got to tell Dr. Lans." Dr. Alan Lans was the team's substance abuse counselor. "He can put you on a good program."

Doc insisted that it had been one time. "Do it and I'll take care of you," he said.

"Oh come on, Doc. I don't want your money." So we did it again.

This time it was a little tougher because the pee guy refused to be distracted. Finally, I screamed at someone and as soon as the tester turned around Doc poured and passed. It worked like a charm.

But again, two weeks after I'd taken the second test, Doc approached me and whispered, "You gotta help me again. He's here." This time I flat-out refused. The only possible reason why Doc wouldn't take the test himself was that he was doing drugs again.

This was a really tough thing for me to do. I told him, "Look, Doc, you got a problem. You've got to get real help."

He didn't answer directly. "I could get suspended," he said, practically pleading.

"Doc, you're my friend. I'm not helping you if I do this. Just pee. If it comes up positive, you just do what you have to." He was pretty angry with me. He took the test and came up positive. He was suspended, and I believe he was fined a substantial amount of money, but he was forced to participate in a treatment program and stopped using.

Obviously, I was really upset that I couldn't take the test for him, but I did what I believed was the right thing to do. I'd had friends who had been addicted to recreational drugs. I knew how they could destroy a person's life. Doc and I didn't speak for the rest of that season, but the following spring we found ourselves alone in the clubhouse. After a long, uncomfortable silence Doc said to me, "Look, I'm sorry I put you in that situation and I'm sorry I got mad at you. Thank you for what you did."

I told Doc the truth: I considered him a friend and would do anything to help him, "But I'm not going to help you hurt yourself. I'm not here to take money from you to do a drug test. I'm worried about you dying. I'm worried about what's going to happen to you if you don't stop now."

Doc offered to pay me as a gesture of appreciation. "Just take care of your problem," I told him. "If I can help you with that, all you gotta do is ask." That was the end of my participation in Doc's drug testing.

I was a fifteen-year-old kid when I started picking up underwear at Shea, and when I finally left I was a twenty-five-year-old man who counted some of baseball's biggest stars among my close friends. I haven't kept a lot of souvenirs from those years, but I still have a few empty champagne bottles—and a few that were never opened—from the locker room celebration after the seventh game of the '86 Series. I still have copies of *Life* magazine that has a photograph of me running onto the field. I have a few scrapbooks. I have some of the special-edition soda cans RC Cola put out. But mostly I have the memories. It may have just been a job, but I certainly got to experience an unbelievable range of emotions as part of a great organization.

When I look back on my days with the Mets, I think the experience may have forced me to grow up too quickly. I missed the normal teenage summers: while my classmates were out at Jones Beach, I was at Shea preparing for games. I was spending my time with adults, and by the time I quit I had absolutely no illusions about professional athletes or major-league baseball. I had no heroes. I knew that every player on the field was a human being, capable of making mistakes, just like me.

I quit working for the Mets in 1995, a few years after Fred Wilpon had bought complete control of the team from Nelson Doubleday. The whole culture was changing at Shea. Where there had once been a large, caring family there was suddenly a restrictive corporate atmosphere. I remember when I started working there we'd been able to give cracked or broken bats to kids in the stands or donate them free of charge to a charity. But after Wilpon took over, everything changed. The staff had to keep a watchful eye on every piece of equipment, on anything that could be sold. Everything from torn batting gloves to cracked bats suddenly had a price. By 1995 it seemed to me that baseball had turned into a cold business that cared only about the bottom line.

Of course, no one will argue with me that baseball has become an enormously profitable industry, for the players as well as the owners. A player in the right situation can sign a contract large enough to support himself and his family—for a few generations. When I started in the game, most players had to work in the off-season just to meet their expenses. But by the time I left the average contract was suddenly close to a million dollars, and a player who might have retired in earlier eras got desperate to play one last season. And maybe one last season after that one.

My value was that I knew how to make that last season possible. Since I was a baseball guy, and had spent years keeping all the secrets, players trusted me. So what started with me just giving advice ended with players coming to me to get what they wanted and needed to compete.

I never imagined it would become a business, that it would end the way it did; after all, these guys were my friends.

THREE

I can't explain it, but from the first day I have always felt at home in a gym. I always felt like it was the place I belonged. I was a scrawny little kid. When I started working out, as a junior in high school, I was lucky if I weighed more than a hundred pounds. I'd hurt my knees playing hockey and one of my friends said, "You gotta start working out and build up your legs." The first gym I went to was near my house, and I didn't have the slightest idea what I was doing. It was an old traditional-type gym designed for people who were serious about body-building. There were no cardio machines or treadmills, no Universal Gym or StairMaster—no modern equipment at all. In fact, the place wasn't even air-conditioned. It was just a place to lift and pound weights. The only equipment it had were weight benches, free weights, and leg machines. It had a real terrible, funky, man smell. And from my first day there I loved it.

I knew it was important for me to build myself up. The men in my family have a history of heart problems—besides my father, two of my uncles died from bad hearts before they were forty. But for me it was more than just a healthy thing to do. I wanted to build up muscle, and I got an incredible feeling of accomplishment when

I saw the results on my own body. I eat healthy, I don't drink, don't smoke, and never did any recreational drugs—even when I was with the Mets and the players around me were doing them. In the gym, I was a natural.

Fortunately, I had some older friends who were into weight training and showed me how to train effectively. I learned all the basics from them. Eventually, we built our own gym in a friend's garage in the Bronx. I contributed some weights I had, another guy gave his weights, and another, who was a welder, made some equipment. What we couldn't build or beg from somebody, we all chipped in to buy, mostly at garage sales. Our gym wasn't beautiful, but it was definitely functional. When the first winter came around, we installed a propane heater so we could continue working out no matter how cold it got. We'd be there after school just about every afternoon.

I began going to real gyms as soon as I got a car, driving up to Westchester where the fees were cheaper. I began meeting a lot of other people who shared my passion. People I knew had started competing in bodybuilding contests, and I learned more about the sport from them. I was becoming obsessed: I read every magazine, talked to all my friends about their personal experiences, and never stopped asking questions. I took everything I learned and experimented with it in my own regimen.

I was training five or six days a week. I loved the high I got from working out. When my blood started flowing, when I started sweating, I'd get into what athletes call "the zone." I was completely focused and feeling great. For me weight training was never about the way I looked. Although I got really cut eventually, I've never done anything to try to impress other people with my physique. In my entire life I've never stood in front of a mirror and admired my body. Actually, it's the opposite: I usually wear loose shirts so people don't know how cut I am.

Soon after I started working out, I discovered that training properly required a lot more than working out every day. In fact, I learned that if I did it too much my body wouldn't grow. Muscles need time to grow without being strained. So I took days off, and as a result I started getting bigger. I was listening to my body. That was probably the first thing I taught baseball players: "You have to listen to your body. Just pay attention and you'll get what you want."

Anabolic steroids were around, but I never even considered using them. It was the rule in the gym that nobody sold or gave anabolic steroids to a teenager, and in fact we were discouraged from using them while we were still growing. Teenagers should not be using anabolic steroids, period. Their natural testosterone—a steroid—is so high that they don't need manufactured steroids to help build their bodies. But my friends and I talked about them all the time. When my more curious friends would try to buy steroids in the gym, people would laugh at them: "Come see me in a couple of years, kid."

I knew a lot of people who were using anabolics. Most people who use them aren't shy about telling you what they think about a given drug. But even then I knew that some of them had no idea what they were talking about. While we were in high school, a couple of my friends got some steroids and started experimenting. They offered some to me but I turned them down. First, because I was afraid of needles—I couldn't even imagine injecting myself—and second, I wanted my body to reach its natural peak before I pushed it artificially.

Instead of using steroids, I learned all about nutrition, about how to structure a workout, about what supplements and other training enhancements were helpful and what others were potentially damaging. I wasn't against steroids, since people I trusted at the gym would talk about them like they were miracle drugs. I knew that eventually I'd try them.

The gym became the focus of my life. When I wasn't in school or at Shea Stadium, I was at the gym. Sometimes after a game, after the clubhouse cleared out, I'd work out there. Around the block from Shea there was a gym that was open twenty-four hours. I'd train there at three o'clock in the morning. I had become obsessed with the sport. I'd put myself on strict diets to see what happened. How would my body react if I ate only so many calories and so much fat? I tried every type of multivitamin supplement from every company. When I was in high school I began drinking protein powders, but every one of them I tried was chalky or cakey and tasted gross, so I started making protein shakes for myself with a little skim milk, different combinations of fresh fruit and juice—and finally the essential ingredient, the protein powder. Once I started making them at Shea, a few players tried them—and some of the players loved them. Soon I was making shakes for players every day. But when our very popular coach Frank Howard tried one, he decided, "This is all right, I guess, but it'd go a lot better with some Jim Beam."

Although I've only competed in one amateur bodybuilding contest, I did go to a lot of shows. I was probably about eighteen years old when I went to my first show. It was an amateur show that was held in a high school auditorium in Mamaroneck, up in Westchester. As soon as I walked into the auditorium a terrible smell hit me. Ironically, bodybuilding is an unhealthy sport. Serious competitors stop drinking water a few days before a show to eliminate all the water between their skin and their muscles so they look really cut. They stop eating properly weeks before. They stuff themselves with proteins and nutrients. Unfortunately, the more protein you take in the more gas you give out. Backstage at a show the smell is overwhelming—everybody is farting.

Several times I got ready for a contest and then, if I wasn't in the mood, didn't go. I never felt the need to prove myself. To prepare for the one show I did participate in, I had to eat, sleep, and shit my body into shape for months before the actual competition. I started dieting sixteen weeks in advance. Every four weeks I'd tweak my diet, limiting fats and meats, and adjusting sodium levels, starches, and simple sugars. In the final four weeks, I cut out all fats and greatly reduced my carb intake. The first time you go on a heavily restricted diet, it's very hard to know how your body will respond. So I paid attention to everything: skin texture, headaches, mood swings, breathing—all aspects of my body were affected. Ten days before, I began reducing my water intake until I reached the point where I was taking no more than two ounces a day. My mouth was so dry I had to suck on lemons to keep from getting chapped. Some guys take diuretics to flush even more water out of their system. By the night of the competition I was so dehydrated I was literally shaking. I was slowly learning what worked efficiently for my body and what created problems.

I did it because I wanted to experience what it was like to train seriously for a competition. I definitely wasn't planning on a career. Like in boxing, bodybuilders compete against people who are about their own size. In the competition I won the tall class, which is comparable to the heavyweight class in boxing. I never competed again. I'd learned that for me the real satisfaction of training came from self-improvement, knowing what I could accomplish with hard work and dedication.

I took my hobby to a different level while I was working for the Mets. Working out to build the best possible physique became a central part of my lifestyle. I was in the gym every day and a lot of my friendships revolved around the gym, so it was a natural progression that personal training became my work. I never decided to do it; it just happened. Before training became my business, I had a lot of other jobs in addition to working for the Mets. In the late eighties and early nineties, I worked for the Mets during the season but through the winter I did construction or put up satellite dishes, whatever I had to do to earn a living. Eventually, though, people who saw me training in the gym started asking me questions about their own workouts.

It started with simple advice. "I'm getting ready for this show. What do you think about . . ." Acquaintances at the gym would ask for diet and workout suggestions, and I'd help them out. Eventually, they began asking me about diets and my recommendations for a complete training program. After giving free advice for a long time, I told people who could afford it that for a few dollars I'd write out a step-by-step exercise and diet program for them. The business grew very quickly.

Most of my initial clients were hard-core bodybuilders who wanted to tone up. I was single at the time, so I'd work with them during the day, go to sleep for a while, and then train myself in the middle of the night. I'd do my own workouts in a twenty-four-hour gym from 4:00 to 6:00 a.m., which I loved because it was nearly always empty. Gradually, my client base expanded to include people who wanted to get in shape or stay in shape. I was working with doctors, lawyers, housewives, even strippers—who I'd train very late at night, after they'd finished working at the clubs.

I had clients ranging from champion bodybuilders to train wrecks. One man started with me when he was fifty-five years old. He smoked, he drank, and he was overweight. As far as his health was concerned, he did everything wrong, and as a result he had a mild heart attack. After being released from the hospital, he started coming to the gym. He didn't have a clue what he was doing. I volunteered to help him, and eventually he insisted on paying me. Over a four-year period, he turned his whole life around. He went from near death to participating in senior bodybuilding shows. My experience with him proved to me that it is never too late to get back into shape and grow muscle.

I'd charge between fifty and two hundred dollars per hour depending on the client. Basically, I'd run around to the different gyms where the clients had memberships. Usually, gyms don't like personal trainers using their facilities—they've got their own people in house. But fortunately I knew the owners of most of the gyms, so I never had to pay.

I loved being a personal trainer. I wasn't digging holes in the snow—one of my other jobs—and I got tremendous satisfaction from seeing people get healthier and improve their bodies. When someone called to tell me they'd lost some weight or received a nice compliment, I felt like I had lost the weight or received the praise. I'm not a traditional personal trainer. I don't have any degrees or certificates. I don't have a personal-training license. But what I do have, and what I shared with my clients, is knowledge and experience. I've seen licensed trainers who barely knew how to use the equipment and understood next to nothing about nutrition and supplements. None of my clients ever asked to see my degree, because they were too busy getting results.

While I was working in the Mets clubhouse, players saw me grow from a skinny kid into a very well-built man. Once I got out of high school, I was training six days a week. During the season, manufacturers would send products for the players to try, and I became the guinea pig. (That way I got my supplements for free.) When I started working in the clubhouse, very few players did any training at all. The accepted theory in the major leagues at that time was that building muscle hurt flexibility, so players were advised to stay away from it. There were a few exceptions: the Phillies' Hall of Fame pitcher Steve Carlton was considered sort of crazy because he practiced martial arts and meditation and did exotic strength and conditioning exercises. One of the strange things he did was bring a large barrel of rice or sand into the clubhouse and work his pitching arm or his legs down to the bottom against tremendous resistance. Players laughed at Greg Jefferies when he admitted that the training regimen set up for him by his father included building strength by swinging a bat underwater. That was about the level of fitness training in the major leagues in the 1980s: punching sand, batting underwater.

At that time, conditioning wasn't taken seriously in baseball. Most of the players would come to spring training badly out of shape, as much as twenty pounds overweight, and they'd need three or four weeks just to lose the weight they gained. At the beginning of spring training, we'd always hand out Mizuno sweat coats and fat-burning rubber waistbands. It was the pitchers, mostly, who would use them. They'd put one on and go running, and within minutes the sweat would be pouring off their bodies. Those coats gave the players who naturally retained water a head start, but using them cost strength and stamina. Instead of building themselves up during spring training, they spent their energy getting their weight down. Every year during that first week of spring training, players would come back to the locker room dying from exertion.

Back then most ballparks didn't even have workout rooms. The Mets turned an empty closet—it was maybe ten feet by fifteen feet—into the training room. It was a dingy space equipped with some weights and old Nautilus equipment. There was no cardio equipment, so it really wasn't much of an improvement over the traditional medicine ball and steam cabinet. But it really didn't matter how big the space was or what equipment was there, since nobody used it anyway. Teams didn't have conditioning coaches or strength coaches at that time, and there was no such thing as a personal trainer anywhere near baseball. Very few players knew anything about nutrition; in fact it was just the opposite. Food was available in the clubhouse like it was a cafeteria. Players could eat junk food from the moment they walked in until they left. It was just too easy to sit there and eat. It wasn't healthy food, either, but sweets and fats. And there were no vitamins, no supplements. Basically, the attitude was that Babe Ruth was fat and it didn't hurt him, right? Some players couldn't resist and ate themselves out of the big leagues.

That giant buffet table wasn't the only unhealthy practice in the clubhouse. When I began working at Shea, I was surprised to find cases of V8 juice in the clubhouse. It was there, I was told by another clubbie, because it was the best known cure for hangovers. I watched the players come in Saturday or Sunday morning, pour themselves a giant glass of V8, add some pepper or hot sauce, and gulp it down. Nasty.

But slowly the players, like the rest of society, started getting interested in nutrition and training. Supposedly, the Phillies' Gus Hoefling became baseball's first strength trainer in the mid-1970s. Gus was one of the nicest people you could meet, but unbelievably tough on players. He was a fifth-degree black belt in karate. When there was free time, he'd come into our clubhouse and teach all the clubbies self-defense moves. He was the one who'd convinced Carlton to use a rice barrel for resistance; he also convinced the Phillies to build a mood room in the basement of Veterans Stadium and introduced the whole concept of mental conditioning. Officially, Hoefling was the Phillies' stretch flexibility instructor, but his success with Carlton made other teams interested in learning more about modern methods of training and conditioning.

The Mets brought in Keith Cedro as their first strength coach at the beginning of the 1987 season. Before that he'd worked in football for the New York Giants. Baseball has always been slow to accept change, so a lot of people thought hiring Cedro was a joke. I heard people seriously say that having muscles never helped any player hit a baseball, and that getting big just slowed them down. Nobody understood that training wasn't about how much weight you could lift but getting into peak condition. Training is a balance between strength and conditioning. Eventually, the Mets added a modern workout room to the clubhouse and equipped it with a LifeCycle, a treadmill, and weights and benches. At that time a team on the road had no access to a workout room or any training equipment, so when we went on the road Keith would pack weights and portable benches into trunks and bring them with us. The clubhouse guys in other cities really disliked him because they had to unpack the trunks. But by the end of the 1980s, the owners agreed to equip every visiting-team clubhouse with two LifeCycles so no one had to carry their own equipment.

While the Mets were among the first teams to provide a well-equipped training facility, most players didn't bother using it. I remember that as late as 1992 Kevin McReynolds, who was getting a bad reputation for being overweight, had to ask Cedro how to operate a LifeCycle, one of the most basic pieces of gym equipment available. Although Straw worked out occasionally, stars like Howard Johnson, John Franco, Dave Magadan, Ron Darling, and Bobby Bonilla never trained. Unfortunately, Doc didn't train either, which I believe hurt him tremendously. He could have played several years more if he'd taken better care of his body. At the beginning of the season, we'd hang weight belts up on hooks for all the players, but at the end of the season Doc's was still hanging there, gathering dust. That was the norm: it was baseball tradition. Not only Babe Ruth but Ted Williams, Mickey Mantle, Willie

Mays—the greatest players in baseball history—never trained, and it didn't seem to affect their game.

I don't think most major leaguers took training very seriously until Oakland's Bash Brothers, Mark McGwire and José Canseco, began hitting home runs. Then players began paying attention. There is a very old saying in baseball, "Home run hitters drive Cadillacs," meaning that power hitters get the biggest contracts. Keith Cedro tried to change the culture of the clubhouse. I did my part to help him by providing MET-Rx protein bars and other healthier alternatives to the usual food choices, and I began making protein shakes for any player who wanted them.

I brought in all the ingredients. I'd spend thirty-five dollars a day when the team was home. I made the most exotic concoctions. I'd mix watermelons, kiwis, oranges, apples, peaches, pears, plums, and grapes with frozen strawberries and raspberries. The Mets had a deal with Tropicana, which provided some wild juices that I threw into the mix. There was no formula. I just experimented until I found something that tasted great. Snapple had just become available and I tried various flavors. I mixed everything with MET-Rx protein powder so the drinks provided extra calories and protein. I got great results: the players loved them. They started to improve their diets. Some guys would have a shake after batting practice rather than the usual five cheeseburgers. The more different types of shakes I made, the more the players wanted them. It was something new. Even if the players didn't understand the nutritional value, my shakes tasted great, gave them an energy boost, and made them feel good. Pretty soon I was making twenty-five to thirty shakes before each game.

The players saw that I was in great shape, so they started asking questions. Baseball wasn't very different from society in general: working out was becoming fashionable and people all around the country were beginning to pay attention to their bodies. I knew that the techniques I had learned in the gym could easily be adapted to baseball, but I didn't say anything. It wasn't my place and it certainly wasn't my job.

When Keith Cedro left the Mets, in 1989, he was replaced by the Yankees' former strength coach, Jeff Mangold. Unfortunately, there were several players who didn't like Jeff. So rather than listen to him, those players would come to me to ask questions about fitness: "What should I eat?" "What supplements should I be using?" "How much sleep should I be getting?" "Can you write me a training program?"

During the regular season, players spend a lot of time just sitting and waiting, and at those times I began having conversations with a few of them about their workout regimens. Every once in a while someone would ask me, "What do you think McGwire and Canseco are doing? Are they taking something?" I don't remember anyone criticizing them; mostly the players just wanted to know what different substances could do for them, how they worked, and if using them was dangerous.

In the late 1980s very few players knew anything at all about steroids and supplements, and nobody had heard of growth hormones. The main thing players used to take was a multivitamin that was available in the clubhouse—and they knew for sure that it worked because it turned their urine a bright yellow and really stank. The drugs players knew about then were cocaine, marijuana, and amphetamines. Steroids were the things that muscular football players used to bulk up to over three hundred pounds, the stuff that track stars used to increase their speed. But most players assumed that steroids didn't have much application to the unique skills required in baseball. So for a long time nobody asked me to get anything for them.

By 1995, when I left the Mets, the attitude about training, conditioning, nutrition, and even steroids had changed completely. The workout rooms, which had been pretty much empty just five years before, were being used all the time. Players would hit the weight room for a half hour or more to get their work in, even after they'd played a full game. With the large salaries they were earning players could afford to work out all winter and report in the spring in better shape than they'd ever been in during the season. The whole climate in baseball had changed. Guys who had been laughing about the new Nautilus equipment four years earlier were going into the weight room to work out on a daily basis. Even Doc was in there sometimes. If you compare spring-training photographs taken in the 1970s and '80s with pictures taken now, you'll see a tremendous difference.

By the mid-1990s every team had a trainer, assistant trainers, and strength and conditioning coaches; they had experts in stretching, chiropractors, and some teams even brought in a yoga instructor and a masseuse. In addition, players were hiring their own personal trainers and nutritionists. Within a couple of years, players were bringing in personal chefs with nutritional expertise.

My friend David Segui and his father, Diego, a pitcher, each played fifteen seasons in the major leagues, and their careers spanned the whole change in attitude about training and fitness in baseball. "My father grew up on a farm in Cuba, swinging a machete," David explains. "He did farm labor by hand. My dad was just naturally strong. He'd laugh at me when I told him I was lifting weights. He told me I was wasting my time. I should get outside and swing an ax. He was old school—he wanted me to chop down trees. That was common with his generation of ballplayers.

"When I first came up to the big leagues in 1990, I had teams telling me not to work out. That I was going to get muscle-bound. But within a couple of years I was working out every day. I got up every morning and did an hour of cardio, lifted a specific body part for maybe thirty minutes, had breakfast or lunch, then got to the ballpark early to do my running. Then after the game I'd lift a half hour for a different body part. And I did this every single day."

From state-of-the-art training rooms to bringing in much healthier food for the buffet tables, teams started focusing on making sure their players were in the best possible physical condition. Players like Roger Clemens, Lenny Dykstra, Randy Myers, and even Sid Fernandez became almost fanatical about getting their workouts in every day. Baseball players got much bigger and much stronger, and some players began searching for anything that might give them the edge.

I quit working for the Mets in 1995 because I wanted to build my own personal-training business. It was almost impossible to establish a good business when I had to spend two months every year in Florida for spring training and be at Shea for eighty-one games a season. And maybe even more importantly, working with the Mets had stopped being fun for me. The Players Association strike, which shut down baseball, convinced me it was time to leave because it signaled that the wonderful days when the Mets organization was an extended family were over.

During the strike, to put pressure on the players to return to work, the owners had brought in scabs, replacement players. I was slipping baseballs to the striking players so they could work out at high schools. I wasn't supposed to do that, but nobody was going to stop me. Some of the replacement players were terrible. One of them had appeared in the movie *Major League,* and he acted like he had actually been in the big leagues. The owners were turning major-league baseball into a joke. I felt that if the owners were willing to make a farce out of the game, I was wasting my time being there. Apparently the fans agreed with me, because after the strike was settled and the major-league players returned, the fans didn't come back. Attendance was way, way down. Baseball desperately needed something to restore interest in the game, and although I couldn't have known it at that time, what they did ended up making all the difference in my life.

It was the home run race between Mark McGwire and Sammy Sosa that first got players interested in bulking up—and using supplements and illegal steroids to do it. Since the morning government investigators showed up at my door, I've tried to remember exactly who the first player I supplied with steroids was. That was one of the first questions Senator George Mitchell asked me. But honestly, I don't know. I understand it's hard to believe that it wasn't a big deal to me, yet that's the truth. I know I should remember who it was, but I don't. After I'd gotten substances for literally hundreds of players, the identities of the first or the second just sort of dissolved into the mix.

My best guess is that the first person I supplied with substances was Lenny Dykstra. I remember when Lenny came up with the Mets in 1985 he was a crazy, rugged, tough kid. He threw his whole body into every game like it was the last one he was ever going to play. Lenny earned his nickname, Nails, because no one played the game harder than him. In the dugout he was unbelievably intense. He couldn't wait to get up, couldn't wait to get out into the field, couldn't wait to be better.

Dykstra was a solid player, not a superstar, but he worked unbelievably hard to take advantage of his talent. He was a little guy, five foot ten, 160 pounds, and a slap hitter, a line-drive hitter. He had no power at all. We became friends in the clubhouse. He'd sit in the players' lounge watching TV while I was working and we'd talk. It was obvious I was into bodybuilding, which he was always curious about, so he'd ask endless questions. We just clicked and became friends, which is why he let me use his sports car when the team was on the road. We didn't spend too much time together away from the ballpark because we had different interests. Lenny was a little wild. He was into drinking; I wasn't. He was into golf; I wasn't. When he was playing for the Phillies, on occasion I'd drive down and after a game we'd go to Atlantic City to play blackjack. Lenny was a much better baseball player than blackjack player. It took him a long time to learn that you can't outhustle the cards.

I believe it was the spring of 1990 when Lenny showed up at Port St. Lucie about thirty-five pounds heavier than he'd been at the end of the last season. I took one look at him and knew what he was doing. But I also knew he was doing it all wrong. He looked puffy, which I knew was both muscle and water. It was obvious to everyone that Lenny was taking something, though not exactly what. People were telling jokes about him. Sometime in the middle of spring training, we sat down and talked about it. "What'd you do?" I asked.

"I'm on the juice," Lenny said. "I want to add some power." He told me that he wasn't looking to hit more home runs. "Hitting thirty home runs and batting .210 isn't going to help me," he said. "But twenty dingers and .290 could get me a good contract."

"What are you taking?" I asked him, although I had a pretty good idea. I just wanted to hear it from him.

He shook his head. "I don't know," he said, and explained that a friend had given it to him and told him how to take it. Lenny was making a pretty common mistake. A lot of people believe all steroids are the same. They're not, because each steroid works differently in your body and has a range of side effects that can mess you up if they aren't used correctly.

"Oh, c'mon, Nails," I said. I was pretty upset with him. "How the fuck could you put shit in your body without knowing what it is? You can't do that, it's crazy. There's lots of ways to take this stuff, but you can't just throw anything into your body. Some of it shouldn't be mixed together."

Lenny didn't believe me. "Look at me," he said, pretty confidently.

But I knew exactly what was going to happen to him. I'd seen it in the gym. "It's nothing. It's just water and you're body isn't going to hold it. When it gets hot, you're gonna shrink like a son of a bitch." I explained to him that he needed to know step-by-step what he was taking. "Some steroids counteract each other, they cancel the effects. You need to know how long to stay on it, whatever it is you're taking, and when to get off it." Lenny smiled that big friendly grin of his and ignored me completely.

Lenny had a great first half of the season. He got exactly what he was looking for. He was driving the ball into the gaps, hitting with a lot more power; his bloopers and soft singles had become hard line drives. The difference was pretty obvious. I didn't tell him, but part of the reason was that he had tremendous confidence, a side effect of steroids. He believed juicing was going to help him, so it did. A hallmark of anabolic steroids is that they give people a kind of Hercules complex. But just as I predicted, when it started heating up in late July and early August, Lenny's weight dropped substantially. He still had a decent season, hitting .270, but during the second half he dropped about twenty-seven pounds, which sapped a lot of his strength and stamina, and he struggled.

During that winter Lenny and I had another conversation about steroids. He was ready to learn more about what they were and how they worked, but at that point he didn't ask me to get anything for him. He had his own guy. That changed a year later, after Lenny had been traded in midseason to the Phillies. At the end of that 1989 season, during which he'd hit only .237 with the worst on-base average of his career while playing for both the Mets and the Phillies, Lenny knew he wanted to start with steroids again. "I have to get back on," he told me. "You know more about it than my guy. Think you could get me something?"

As far as I remember, that's the way it started for me, doing a favor for a friend. "Yeah, I could put something together for you if you want."

Lenny agreed, so I put a whole regimen together for him. We met at the Carlyle hotel in New York and went over all the details. I explained what I was giving him and how to inject it. I emphasized to him that if he wanted to get the best results he had to continue working out. I educated him. I sold him two cycles (a cycle is the period of time you're actually taking juice), and I showed him step-by-step how to break what I was giving him into weekly doses. The following season he got unbelievable results, raising his average ninety-eight points, hitting .325, and increasing his on-base percentage one hundred points.

Lenny and I would meet whenever he came into the city. We'd have lunch or I'd go the ballpark, and we'd sit and talk and I'd make sure he was following up on everything. If we hadn't talked in a while, he would call me just to keep up. Lenny was the kind of guy who would call at three o'clock in the morning and ask, "What are you doing?"

"I'm sleeping, Lenny."

"Oh, man, I can't sleep."

"Lenny, go to sleep. Please," I'd beg him. The problem with Lenny was that he lived life with the same intensity that he played baseball. For him too much was never enough. Lenny never took care of himself. If a candle had three ends, he would have burned all of them. Between the steroids, the amphetamines, and the alcohol, Lenny was a walking pharmacy. Frankly, it was amazing he was able to play as long as he did. He was the ultimate wild man.

To make his situation just a little tougher, Lenny also had serious back problems. Even when he was young he walked with a slouch. People used to think it was just his cocky attitude, but it was caused by a degenerating spine condition. Lenny literally couldn't stand up straight. He even used to bat hunched over. Considering his physical problems, the things he was able to do on a baseball field were pretty amazing. All along Lenny knew how bad his back was. I remember he told me once, "I've got a window of opportunity, a short window, and I need to take advantage of it. When my body's done, it's done." And with the help of steroids, Lenny took advantage of that time, signing one of those multimillion-dollar contracts that ensured his financial security for the rest of his life. But eventually his back just gave out on him.

So for me all this trouble began with Lenny. Or at least I think so. As far as I was concerned, what I did to help him was no big deal. I was simply doing a favor for a friend. I was using my knowledge and experience to help him do his job to the best of his ability. I would have done exactly the same thing for a friend from the gym or from one of the jobs I had in the winter. The concept that it might become a business absolutely never occurred to me. But I was about to find out exactly how many friends I had.

FOUR

When the full extent of my involvement in baseball's steroid scandal was revealed, I know a lot of people wondered exactly who I was and how I had become an expert in the use of steroids, human growth hormones, supplements, and the variety of other substances that players used to try to gain the elusive competitive edge. The answer is easy: I learned all about this stuff because my passion for training brought me to a place where juice is common, a place where people knew all about it and didn't hesitate to talk: the gym.

It's impossible to spend time in a gym—I mean a gym, not one of the modern fitness centers where often the weights only go up to fifty pounds—and not learn about steroids. It's impossible for a bodybuilder or weight lifter to compete at the top level without using steroids and, eventually, human growth hormones. Even the few women that worked out used them. People who are not using them can't compete against people who do. They have no chance. Through the years I collected a tremendous amount of information. Much in the way baseball fans learn about Roger Maris's home run record, I learned about the different steroids and other performance-enhancing substances.

Bodybuilders are the experts on this stuff, since most of them have learned from experience everything they need to know about it. These men are totally dedicated to achieving perfection with their bodies, and many of them are willing to experiment with their own lives to try to get better results. Most hard-core bodybuilders aren't worried about long-term effects; they're driven by what they look like today.

A bodybuilding gym is like a substance laboratory. It's possible to buy steroids at most of the real bodybuilding gyms in America. When a company introduces a new anabolic product, everybody wants to try it. In the gyms I've gone to, nobody was afraid of using steroids, and admittedly sometimes they used too much. I know from my own experience that steroids can be very dangerous when they're used irresponsibly. I have friends who have abused their bodies so badly I still don't understand why they're alive. I had one terrifying experience several years ago: I was training with a friend and suddenly blood started spurting from his nose. I'd seen it happen before—he'd burst a blood vessel. We tried to pack it with gauze to stem the flow, and when that didn't work we put ice packs on it. But nothing would stop the bleeding. After thirty minutes we rushed him to the emergency room. Fortunately, we got there just in time—the doctors barely saved his life. They shot a balloon up his nose to stanch the bleeding. Only later did I find out that he had high blood pressure and his cholesterol level was through the roof—but he still was shooting steroids into his body.

A lot of serious bodybuilders even make their own steroids. They become chemists in their own homes, buying whatever supplies they need to make their own extra-strength testosterone. Their theory is that more is better, which people have learned is not necessarily true. In fact, the real danger of any of these substances generally comes from using too much. At the levels ballplayers were using steroids, there was absolutely no danger. Unfortunately, there are bodybuilders who don't care and continue to experiment with anything they can get their hands on. Often it's not even a new product, just a different blend. For example, instead of making a shot of testosterone 100 milligrams (mg) per cubic centimeter (cc), they're making it 400 or 500 mg per cc. A company can create a new product by using less oil or by mixing substances together to create a new steroid. Essentially, as soon as a new product is available, people start trying it and everybody at the gym wants to know about the results.

Personally, I used both anabolics and later growth hormones for many years. I would do a cycle: three or four months on, then nothing for the rest of the year. I watched people using these substances and instructed people in how to use them, and neither I nor my clients ever had a bad experience. Admittedly, there can be serious problems. Any water-based steroid can cause a bacterial infection, so you have to be careful; you have to know what you're doing and pay attention. Bacteria will grow in water and can cause a very unpleasant reaction. In fact the only death I could ever attribute to steroid use happened because a bodybuilder made the terrible mistake of using the same needle to inject himself several different times. That was absolutely unnecessary because pins, as we refer to needles, are easily available. But this person reused the same needle, which eventually got contaminated and caused a staph infection that traveled to his heart and led to his death.

I would bet that pretty much anything that could be done with steroids has been tried. People inject themselves in their calves, their triceps, their shoulders, or any part of their body to see if they can get better results. Substances sold in pill form are not supposed to be injected, but some people would crush the pills, heat them up to purify them, and then inject them to avoid processing them through their livers. That's dangerous, but if there was even a chance of improved results there were always people willing to take the risk.

Juice is an essential part of the training culture. I can walk into any gym and just by looking around know who is using steroids and, most of the time, have a pretty good idea what they're using. It's no mystery because most steroids have obvious physical effects. Some of them cause users to retain water, others eliminate water and make you look cut, and others cause acne. In fact, not only do I know who's using them, but within a few days I know what substances are available, who's selling them, and how much they cost.

Back then, the unspoken rule was that you didn't bring steroids into the gym itself and never used them in the gym. The owners of the gyms generally knew what was going on, but as long as they weren't being used in the gym, or sold inside the gym, they didn't care. People didn't even like talking about it while working out there. Selling steroids to people you meet at the gym is not like selling recreational drugs. It's not nearly as profitable. Maybe the people bringing them into the country are making decent money, but most of the people in the gym who sell them use their profits to pay for their own personal supply. Using steroids can be very expensive. One cycle—a cycle can range from six weeks to thirty weeks—can cost as much as five thousand dollars.

I used steroids for the first time when I was twenty-one years old. One of my friends got a bottle and we split it. Initially, I used testosterone and Deca-Durabolin. But before I took them, I had done my homework so I knew what to expect. I was over two hundred pounds and my body was still growing. The first time I experimented I did a small cycle, about eight to ten weeks long. During that time I gained thirty-five pounds. When I stopped I lost about twenty of those pounds, leaving me with fifteen pounds of new muscle.

Steroids were illegal at that time, but they hadn't been designated as a controlled substance, requiring triple script from doctors—meaning having them in your possession without a valid doctor's prescription is a felony—as they are now, so they were relatively easy to get, but still very expensive. There are some people who stay on them all year and spend as much as thirty thousand dollars. The cost isn't only the price of the drug. It's everything else that you should be doing at the same time—you need to be eating right; you want to make sure you're getting enough protein; and you should be taking supplements. Using steroids the right way can be very expensive, but doing it any other way is a waste of money.

For me the effects were dramatic, psychologically as well as physically. I felt invincible. As I got stronger I felt much better about myself. I had been bench-pressing two hundred pounds, but suddenly I was getting up to three hundred. My self-esteem was way up, which is a very common side effect. As with some recreational drugs, the first time I used them the results were just staggering, but, like everyone else, I found that each time I used them the results were a little less noticeable. I probably used steroids for twelve years. I experimented with all the various types that were available. I got to know what did what, when to use them, how much to use. I'm the type of person who writes everything down, so I bought a notebook and kept track of the effect that every drug I did had on my body, and later I would encourage players to do the same thing. Eventually, I filled more than two hundred pages. I kept a daily record at the bottom of each page including everything I ate that day, how much sleep I'd gotten, what type of workout I did, what substances I used, and how I felt. If I had a good day, I'd put a star on the page; for a bad day, I'd put a mark. A bad day meant I'd felt weak in the gym or that I'd lost my focus. Gradually, that's how I learned what my body needed. I noticed that some days I got all the sleep I needed but I still didn't feel right. I'd see that that day I had tweaked my diet: I'd ingested fewer carbs or less fat, maybe only twenty grams less, than the day before when I'd earned a star. So I'd experiment the next day to see if I correctly identified the aspect of my regimen that had caused that difference.

I began using anabolic steroids regularly, mostly Deca and testerone, and not in large amounts—just enough to give me the edge. I wasn't sure if I wanted to compete again, but I wanted to get bigger. That was my objective: getting bigger. I just needed a push to help me reach my goals. I was growing and growing and I felt great. Even when I was juicing regularly, I never stayed on steroids for long periods of time. I would go through a twelve-week cycle then stay off for months.

Most people only have some sort of vague understanding of what steroids do. One thing they don't do is turn ordinary players into superstars. If taking steroids was some kind of magic potion, Mr.

Olympia would be in the Baseball Hall of Fame. The proof of this is the Giambi brothers. Both Jason and his brother Jeremy were major leaguers who took roughly the same substances. Jason has been a slugging star for more than a decade; Jeremy never really made it and only played parts of six big league seasons. There was a clubhouse joke based on the fact that steroids were easily available in Mexico: if steroids really make players better, why hasn't Texas won a World Series?

There are about a dozen different types of steroids available, and various companies produce different formulations of each one of them. But none of them can help a player hit a curveball or throw a split-fingered fastball. Major leaguers reach that level because of their talent, not because of the drugs they take. For example, Darryl Strawberry didn't use steroids, and I've never seen a player who was using them hit a ball farther than him. Straw's problems were recreational drugs and alcohol, not steroids. Several of my clients were minor-league players. I got them what they needed and they took it, and they remained minor-league players. Steroids enabled them to perform to the level of their ability every day—but their ability wasn't good enough.

Steroids enable you to build muscle, but only if you work out. I always told my clients that if they weren't going to work out and follow my instructions, then they shouldn't waste my time and their money because they weren't going to achieve any meaningful results. When you stop training, you lose whatever weight you had gained. I knew guys in the gym who started taking steroids and expected to get a body like the champions in the training magazines. I actually had a client who brought in a page he'd torn out of a magazine and told me that was the body he wanted, like I was a plastic surgeon. I told him I was a personal trainer, not a miracle worker. I explained that if he wanted a body like the one in the magazine, he had to work incredibly hard and get new parents. Steroids can do a lot, but they can't change your genetic makeup. The true benefit is recuperation. In baseball, players often have great first halves of the season but in the second half they're dead. That's because their body just breaks down. Anabolics would allow them to work out more and gain muscle. The muscle they added helped them hit the ball harder; it turned singles into doubles and helped ballplayers perform at their top level for the whole season.

I'm not a chemist: I don't know the chemical makeup of steroids. I don't know the physiology of how they work—but I know what they do and how to use them. I know about all the different types of steroids and when to use each one of them and how much to take. I know specifically what each steroid does to your body. Anabolic steroids build muscle mass, increase strength, promote bone growth, and increase your appetite.

Steroids were first identified, isolated, and produced in a laboratory in the 1930s. Long before they were discovered by baseball players, steroids were commonly used by athletes in other sports. They first made headlines after the 1952 Olympics. Supposedly, the Russian weight lifting and wrestling teams were given testosterone injections before the games, and when they won numerous medals everybody started getting interested in them. In 1956 the American company Ciba Pharmaceuticals created Dianabol and Methandrostenolone, the first synthetic steroids that were not testosterone. After that people started experimenting with them in all sports. Before the 1972 Olympics, American weight lifter Ken Patera, who was about to compete with the legendary Russian Vasily Alexeev, pretty much summed up reality when he admitted, "When I hit Munich next year we'll see which are better—his steroids or mine."

As athletes have proven, steroids can translate into big dollars. And as long as that remains true, athletes are going to find a way to use them. In America steroids turned out to be the perfect drug for football players, who need to build bulk in addition to agility and stamina. The use of various substances in pro football had been an open secret in the NFL for decades. The average NFL career is only about four years. The teams push the players to get every ounce out of them before their bodies give out. Trainers will give them whatever they need to get them back on the field. That means not only steroids but cortisone, painkillers, amphetamines—anything that gets them back in the game. To be successful in professional football, players definitely have to abuse their bodies. Not least because 350 pounds is too much weight for a body to carry. In 1987 the NFL passed its first antisteroid policy, but anybody who believes that stopped their use hasn't been watching those 350-pound linemen run down those 200-pound running backs. Professional football can wipe out a body; I've seen players after they retire and some of them can barely walk. The game has crippled them. I've talked to many active pro football players over the years. I'd run into them at gyms or at charity functions, and a few of the New York players would come by the Mets camp during spring training. I remember asking one of them, "Don't you worry about being tested?" He laughed. Literally, he laughed.

He told me that NFL players have some idea of when they are going to be tested, though he didn't tell me how they know. "It's not as random as people think," he said, adding that it really wasn't a big problem, "because they're not looking to break balls."

I know anabolics are being used in pro basketball because I supplied an NBA player for several years. He had grown up in the same town as a major leaguer, and as a favor to that person I met this NBA player for dinner and we talked about it. He told me that other players were using them and he was curious. Talking to professional athletes about steroids was like discussing investments with bankers. It was completely dispassionate, because most of them just wanted as much information as possible. Every serious athlete had heard the rumors about what steroids could do for them—as well as the dangers. To my knowledge, steroids weren't used as extensively in pro basketball as they were in football or baseball. A lot of NBA players didn't seem to know that much about steroids or what they could do for them. This player wanted to increase his endurance. He used them to keep his legs fresh. The NBA schedule is as tough as major-league baseball's, and basketball is an unbelievably physical game. In addition to all the running they do, NBA players take a beating. Pro basketball is a full-contact sport, and the guys they're playing against are as big and tough as they are. The running, the physical contact, and even the lifestyle together result in tremendous wear and tear on ankles, knees, and hips.

So long before baseball players got interested, steroids were being used in several other sports. In fact for a long time most baseball people didn't appreciate their potential benefits. Size and strength have never been considered a particular advantage in baseball. Bigger hitters have a larger strike zone, which makes it easier to pitch to them, and a 320-foot home run is worth exactly the same amount of runs as a 400-foot shot. For pitchers strength doesn't necessarily translate to a livelier fastball. The general consensus in baseball was that using steroids would not be a big benefit to the players.

I remember when I realized that this was about to change. One day in 1990, I went to a game at Yankee Stadium and saw José Canseco and Mark McGwire walk by, about fifty feet away. The person I was with, who also knew a lot about juice, asked me, "What do you think?"

"You're kidding, right?" As soon as I saw Canseco and McGwire, I knew what they were doing. I could see it by the color and the texture of their skin. I had no doubt about it. I hadn't thought very much about it before, but knowing the lifestyle of major leaguers and the demands of the season I could see how baseball players could benefit from steroids. Still, I didn't mention it to anyone.

When I first began helping out players, I had no intention of becoming a supplier. By that time most major leaguers who were juicing had their own sources they trusted. Instead, as I've said, they called me to ask questions about conditioning, nutrition, and even sleep problems. They wanted me to help them set up workout routines. That's how it began: I made out complete diet and training routines for numerous players—and, at the beginning, always without being paid.

Eventually though, after McGwire, Canseco, and Sosa put up huge numbers, my guys began asking me about steroids. The players were very curious since it had become obvious that using steroids could give them a big edge. I got endless questions, like

"What do you think he's using?" "Do you think I should use this?" "How much of that stuff is it safe to take?" "I'm getting tingling in my fingers, what does that mean?" Pretty soon, I was the answer man. One first baseman told me that he realized he had to find out more about steroids when "I was standing on first base next to the other team's shortstop—and he was twenty pounds heavier than me. It made me feel very insecure. That's the day I got curious."

McGwire, Canseco, and Sosa were the players who originally made other major leaguers look seriously at the value of steroids. But it was after the extraordinary success of Barry Bonds that almost everybody in the big leagues realized they needed to learn everything possible. By then the use of steroids and "growth" had become common and generally accepted in the major leagues. I never had anything to do with Bonds, but I had asked some people questions about him and it came back to me that he was working "with a guy just like you."

Other players saw what steroids did for Bonds, and particularly when they saw the size of his salary and the fact that baseball didn't seem to be upset by his obvious drug use, they wanted to know more about these substances. I can't even estimate how many players asked me if I knew what he was using, what the long-term effects would be, and what results they might get from the same.

I told them all the same thing: "He's definitely doing growth, and probably anabolics too, because he's growing too fast. You just don't build that kind of muscle unless you're using anabolics." But I pointed out that everybody is different and that every player couldn't expect to get results like Bonds. "Your body is different from anybody else's. Your max may be two hundred pounds. You have to learn about your own body." Bonds was pushing the limits, I told them, because it was obvious to anyone, just by looking at him, that he was on the juice. It looked like somebody had stuck a pump into Barry Bonds and blown him up with muscle. The fact that it was so obvious defeated the whole purpose of it—which was doing it without anybody knowing that you were juicing.

At the time, most major-league players were confident that baseball knew what was going on. And the implied message was that if baseball was going to allow Bonds and McGwire and Canseco to get away with it, why shouldn't they do it? There didn't seem to be a real downside. Unlike recreational drug use, for which a few well-known players had been suspended for life—some of them several times—there had been no similar penalties for steroid use. The Players Association had successfully built a wall of regulations to protect the players from being tested or penalized, and baseball didn't fight them very hard. It had already shown that it had no intention of taking any serious actions. In 1991 the commissioner, Fay Vincent, had specifically included steroids in the policy that prohibited the use of any prescription drugs without a legitimate prescription. Nobody cared, nobody paid attention, nobody changed their routine. The general feeling was that baseball had to put that rule on the books to please the public but wouldn't actually enforce it. Not as long as attendance kept rising. It seemed like the message was pretty obvious: if it isn't cocaine, it's part of the game.

I remember I was sitting behind two scouts during a game in 1994 and listening to them go through the lineups and speculate about which players were using juice. "This guy must be juicing up. What do you think about that guy?"

I didn't know everything that was going on inside baseball—the use of performance-enhancing substances was too widespread for anyone to know it all—but I certainly was as knowledgeable as anyone else. I had to be, because I was one of the primary people educating the players. I can't put myself in the minds of the players to figure out why so many of them decided to use steroids, but still a sizeable number made the opposite decision. I know several players who told me they had to use them just to keep up with the competition. In 2002, after Ken Caminiti admitted his own steroid use, Paul Lo Duca tried to bring a little reality to the situation, telling a reporter, "If you're battling for a job and the guy you're battling with is using steroids, then maybe you say, 'Hey, to compete I need to use steroids because he's using them.' Don't get me wrong, I don't condone them. But it's a very tough situation. It's really all about survival for some guys."

A few players called me to talk about performance-enhancing substances but never called again. Maybe they had another source or decided against using them. But I also met a lot of players like retired pitcher Dave LaPoint, who would ask me, kiddingly I suspect, "Where were you when I was at the end of my career? If I knew you then I could have been set for life."

But usually, by the time players called me they had already made the decision to give them a try. They wanted to know every aspect: what to take, how much to take, and even how to take it. While it sounds simple, getting the most benefit from steroids can be complicated. There are at least a hundred different anabolics used in weight training, ranging from clenbuterol to Winstrol, but for athletes there are only about ten or twelve common steroids that can provide meaningful effects. Each has a very different effect on the body and offers specific benefits when used correctly. Most steroids will give you additional strength, but some will give you more than others; some will give it to you faster than the others, some work best under certain conditions, and some require dietary restrictions. Some will make you hold water, and others carry more oxygen to increase stamina. Some of them will help you heal quicker. Not only is every one of them different, every brand of each steroid has a different makeup by percentage. Over time I learned it all. I learned by asking questions at the gym: How'd the Quality Vet (QV) stuff work? Animal Power? Did you use the yellow tops or the other ones? Did this one hold water better than that one? Did you get the strength you wanted when you took that? By the time I got involved with baseball players, I knew what to recommend in almost every situation.

At first everybody in baseball used Deca-Durabolin, Deca for short. It's probably the most popular steroid; bodybuilders love it because it builds muscle slowly—so it almost looks like natural growth—while increasing joint fluid, making it easier to lift heavy weights. Deca helps relieve the soreness in shoulders and joints; it's particularly good for reducing the impact of groin injuries. For pitchers, Deca is particularly great for increasing strength and reducing some of the stress on the elbow joint. It builds muscle, but not so much that it begins to affect flexibility. It doesn't even produce particularly noticeable side effects; the only thing that made some players a little squeamish is that you have to inject it. But initially it seemed like everybody who called me wanted Deca: "Deca. Get me some Deca." In fact, it was so common that the name almost became a synonym for steroids.

The problem with Deca is that it's oil based, which means traces of it are detectable in your body for as long as eighteen months after you inject it, sometimes even longer. When baseball began its testing program in 2003, I told players they needed to switch to water-based substitutes, since those drugs can be out of your system as quickly as fourteen days, making them more difficult to detect. If players knew when they were going to be tested—and despite baseball's claim that testing was random I was told by several players that they had been warned when they were going to be tested—it was easy to figure out when to take a water-based steroid and when to stop in order to make sure you pissed clean.

After baseball's testing program started, players mostly began using substitutes like Propenate, Anavar, Primobolan, and Winstrol. Propenate, for example, is very fast acting; your system will absorb it in six to eight hours, but the problem is that anything that your body absorbs that quickly is going to make you sore. Propenate manufacturers would claim the bottle contained 50 mg while they really put in 100, so people who took it would be sore for two or three days. And it hurt. I remember warning a player that taking Propenate would definitely be painful, but he didn't listen to me. He called me later, laughing, and admitted, "You weren't kidding. After I took the shot, my ass was on fire."

With slower-acting steroids there is no pain at all. Anavar is probably the mildest steroid, and while it doesn't produce the same results as most of the alternatives, Anavar will build some muscle and reduce fat. It comes in pill form and its big advantage is that while these changes take time they're permanent. Even after you stop taking it, the weight you've lost stays off and the muscle you've gained remains. The downside of Anavar is that because it is mild you've got to take a lot of it to realize the benefits.

Primobolan is also a mild steroid, but it wasn't really convenient for ballplayers. In order to get the full effect, a complete cycle takes as long as twelve weeks, which can difficult for a ballplayer who spends nearly half the season on the road.

The benefit of Winstrol is that it's very effective and can stay in your body for two or three weeks, so it was very popular. It was the first choice of a lot of players, and unfortunately it was the steroid David Segui was using when he tested positive.

I met pitcher Denny Neagle before he joined the Yankees. By that time he had already won twenty games and been an All-Star. The first time he called me, he didn't hesitate to discuss his own steroid use. "I'm using Winstrol," he told me. Winstrol was particularly popular among pitchers because it helped reduce fat without a corresponding loss of stamina. Winstrol also carries extra oxygen to your blood so you don't get winded. But I warned him, "I wouldn't use that. There are other things that are better for you. The problem with Winstrol is that it's just not great when it starts getting hot in August. Winstrol will dehydrate you. You're gonna sweat all the water out of your system. Everything is going to get too tight and you could pop a hamstring. You could have shoulder problems, elbow problems . . ."

I don't think Neagle believed me. "I like Winstrol," he said. "I've had a lot of success with it so I'm going to keep using it." We had a friendly disagreement. Literally two days later, two days, I was watching the game on television. He rounded third base and all of a sudden he grabbed at his hamstring. He could barely make it to home plate. The next day I got a call from him. "How the fuck did you know that?"

"I told you why," I said. "Heat and humidity are the enemies when you're taking Winstrol." After that day, Neagle did whatever I told him. Believe me, this is really what was going on behind the scenes of major-league baseball. There was a lot of posturing about drug use and drug testing and baseball cleaning up, but conversations like that one took place every day.

Eventually Denny Neagle and I became friends, and I began supplying him with growth hormones and occasionally a steroid. At the end of the 2000 season, he signed a five-year, fifty-one-million-dollar contract with the Rockies. After that we'd meet each time he came to New York. We'd have lunch at T.G.I. Friday's or Ruby Tuesday, and I'd give him whatever he needed. Those exchanges weren't done in secret: it was all out in the open. That's the way baseball was back then. Over time, Neagle struggled with injuries; I'm sure the growth hormones I sold him helped him stay in the game, but he never regained the success he'd had earlier in his career.

He introduced me to a few of his friends. One of them was a trainer who called me often to discuss legal supplements. He wanted to know what I was recommending, for what purpose and why. I spent many hours on the phone with this friend and never made any money. But that wasn't the point. For me this was my passion. This was my human laboratory.

Neagle certainly wasn't the only player who didn't listen to my advice. I'm sad to say that I couldn't stop Ken Caminiti from abusing steroids. Caminiti, the first real star to admit publicly that he had used steroids, died of a heart attack in 2004, when he was only forty-one years old. Caminiti's confession certainly didn't surprise me, since we'd spoken a couple of times. He had been a very good player; in 1996—the year he claimed he had started taking steroids—he was the National League's Most Valuable Player. He told the media he had started taking steroids because he was trying to recover from a shoulder injury. Okay, if that's what he said.

I spoke with Caminiti twice: once we sat by his locker at Shea and the second time, a couple of seasons later, in the runway between the dugout and the clubhouse. By that time a lot of players knew that I was knowledgeable about training and all the substances people were using, so even players that I didn't know at all would stop me and ask me questions. It was well known in baseball that Caminiti had a serious drinking problem to go with everything else he was doing. Later he admitted that he was also doing cocaine, and after his retirement he spent time in rehab. Caminiti, I think, was the perfect example of someone willing to sacrifice his future for the present. When we spoke, he wanted to ask me questions about the steroid he was taking. When he told me he was taking Anadrol, I knew he was in trouble. Anadrol is the strongest steroid available, an old-school drug that really isn't used very often anymore. It's an instant fix—but with huge results come dangerous consequences. It makes your whole body practically explode with muscle. It's popular among bodybuilders at the beginning of a cycle to get them going, to bulk up, but they replace it pretty quickly with a less toxic steroid. It will make you strong within a week. You can put on twenty pounds in two weeks, if you don't mind destroying your liver and risking jaundice, cancer, and all the potential dangers of high blood pressure. Anadrol is particularly brutal on your liver. It's like pouring acid on it. It burns holes in your stomach. There's no real reason for anybody to be taking it unless they're under strict medical supervision. It's prescribed by doctors for the treatment of anemia caused by an inability to produce red blood cells. And it's essential that you take it for only a very short period of time.

"How long have you been on it?" I asked.

"Just a few weeks," he said, and told me that he was suffering from diarrhea and bad stomach cramps. "Is that normal?"

Normal? "You're killing yourself," I told him. Anadrol by itself is devastating to the liver, but add alcohol to it and you've got no chance. "Listen, man," I said, "you keep doing this and you're not going to live long." I told him he needed to stop taking it immediately and get some help.

He didn't hear me. He told me that it was just a temporary thing, that he'd been doing it for a while with no adverse effects.

To me getting stomach cramps, destroying your liver, and putting up with diarrhea are pretty adverse effects, but obviously Caminiti was in denial. He admitted to me that he was hesitant to quit because when he ended a cycle, when he stopped taking the steroid, he'd come crashing down hard. "I'm having these mood swings," he said.

Like with several other players, I could almost track Caminiti's use by the numbers he put up. His bat would be on fire for a few weeks, and then he'd end the cycle and a week later his numbers would come way down. Caminiti wanted to know how to counteract that effect and try to maintain a more even performance. I told him there were some things that he could do that would help and we discussed them. Some of them he knew about, like milk thistle, which alcoholics use to clean out their livers, and supplements, but he wanted more information. What bothered me was that he had some knowledge about the subject, so he knew the physical risks that he was taking. He had accepted those risks in return for the rewards. For him it was worth sacrificing his long-term health to stay at the top of his game.

When we stood there on the runway, we could just as easily have been two plumbers talking about pipe fittings. That's how casual it was. Caminiti's teammates strolled by, and the few that I knew nodded a greeting, but I got the feeling that at least some of them knew what we were talking about. They knew what Ken was doing and they knew my background. For me, at least, my concern wasn't that he was doing something illegal—that didn't even occur to me—but I was worried about him.

It was obvious that he was in real danger, and what it made even more dangerous for him was that he was getting the results he wanted to get. The stuff he was taking worked for him. He was a productive player earning a very good salary and was well-liked in baseball. The only downside was that what he was doing could kill him. I believe Caminiti was completely aware of the risks and, like other addicts, he thought he could stop using when he needed to, so he accepted them.

I remember walking away that second time, shaking my head. I took great pride in making sure anything that I provided for some-one was going to be used safely. Caminiti never asked me to get product for him and I never offered. But whoever he was getting his stuff from obviously hadn't taken the same precautions as I did.

Because injecting steroids should be done in a very specific way to avoid creating cysts, I had to teach a lot of my clients how to do it. Believe me, I gave the same spiel so many times I know it by heart. "Have you taken shots before?" Yeah, sure, everybody had. "Where?" My arm, my ass, you know. "Okay, here's the easiest advice I can give you. The best place to take anabolics is in your behind. If you take it in your shoulder, you're going to get sore in that area. So go ahead and look at your ass in the mirror. Pick out one cheek. Now in your mind break it up into four equal areas; make a cross section, two on top, two on the bottom. Now just stay in the middle, where the lines cross. You don't want to go too low because you'll hit your sciatic nerve, and you don't want to go too high because there are too many things to hit up high. You want to stay in the middle. You can hit the top of that line or the bottom of that line; go from left to right and you'll be fine. Then switch cheeks. Don't hit the same spot or you're going to build up scar tissue. You want to switch from side to side. There are two shots a week and you want to alternate so one side's not getting two shots in the same week."

I reminded them that there were a lot of books available that would give them step-by-step instructions on how a person could give themselves a shot. I also told them where they could find instructions on the Internet. I emphasized how important it was that they not hit the same spot too often. I knew guys in the gym who had built up so much scar tissue they could barely take an injection. Without physically standing next to them to demonstrate the technique, I found my speech was the best way to explain it to them. Only once did I actually inject a player. One day in the Mets clubhouse, reliever Josias Manzanillo pulled me aside and started asking me questions. He said he had something he wanted to show me. He showed me a bottle, and I immediately knew what it was. "Where do I take this?" he asked.

"Well, you could take it in your shoulder with a small pin or take it in your butt with a larger one." He had a small needle. He was right-handed so I told him, "Take it in your left shoulder. You don't want a sore shoulder at the injection site."

"Do me a favor," he asked. "Could you show me?"

We went into a small storage room. I locked the door and gave him the shot, showing him with each step how he should do it himself. That was it. I didn't think it was a big deal, and we never talked about it again. It was the kind of thing that people do for friends in the gym every day. Josias never asked me to get anything for him. So obviously he had his own source. Actually, I taught quite a few players how to inject themselves. I remember going through it with David Segui. I led them through it like I was teaching a kindergarten class. This is how you draw it out of the bottle; this is how you push it into your tissue. While nobody minded getting an injection from their doctor, since we've all been getting shots our whole lives, only a few players were really comfortable sticking themselves with a needle for the first time. It definitely was a psychological barrier that many players had to overcome. But once they got over that reluctance and understood how easy it was, there was no problem. In fact many players were surprised the process was so simple. How could you get such incredible results from something that easy?

Players loved the fact that I was a one-stop shop: when a player told me precisely what results he was looking for, whether it was more power, more stamina, or a few more miles per hour on his fastball, I could put together a program that would help him achieve those goals. And not only would I supply the steroids or growth hormones at a fair price, I would teach them how to use the substance safely and warn them about the potential side effects. When they needed me, I was always available to help them. Unlike my failure with Caminiti, some players who were thinking about using a steroid that was wrong for them listened to me when I explained that they should be using something else, or, as with some of my gym clients, that steroids really weren't right for them.

I believe, and I've always told people, that steroids shouldn't be used by everyone. Each person is different and should be treated as a unique individual. Obviously, major-league players are in very good physical condition, but even they have to be aware of the potential problems. All steroids elevate your blood pressure and cholesterol level. They also cause acne and bloating, which are the recognizable signs of someone who has taken them. So if a person is overweight, out of shape, and has high cholesterol or really high blood pressure, the reality is that taking steroids could cause a heart attack.

In addition to the physical risks, there definitely are psychological side effects to juicing. The mood swings that Caminiti mentioned are probably the best-known side effect of steroids. It's absolutely a fact that in addition to the obvious physical effects there are less-obvious psychological effects. One of the first questions a player would inevitably ask was if steroids were addictive. I would tell them that in my experience they weren't addictive in the same physiological way nicotine, caffeine, alcohol, or certain drugs were addictive, meaning that your body didn't become physically dependent on them and react violently when you stopped using it. But steroids were addictive psychologically.

When someone is on a cycle, they feel so good and productive that they want to sustain that feeling—sort of like smokers who use cigarettes to reduce stress. It isn't too hard to figure out that if you're feeling great you want to continue feeling great, and you want to maintain that feeling as long as possible. In fact one of the more common psychological effects was self-confidence. In some cases the juice worked because people believed it worked. I've had people in the gym take it for the first time and two days later tell me with wonder, "This is the greatest thing that I've ever seen. I can bench twenty pounds more than I've ever done before."

Maybe that was true, but it wasn't because of the physical impact of the steroids. In those cases the increased performance was caused by the power of the mind, since these substances don't have an effect until several days after you've started taking it. But if you believe it works, that psychological strength is just as real as the steroids. In every sport, as in life, confidence is a vital component of success.

Probably the best known of the side effects of steroid use is so-called roid rage, which is described as an uncontrollable outburst of anger and violence—with sometimes superhuman strength—that supposedly happens, as part of the withdrawal, after you've stopped using them. There have been several attempts to blame roid rage for assaults, murders, and suicides. I've heard a story that some FBI agents believe that roid rage caused O. J. Simpson to kill Nicole Simpson and Ron Goldman. Supposedly, he'd been taking steroids to look buff for a movie, *The Frogman*, he'd finished shooting a couple of weeks before the killings, and when he saw his ex-wife with a man he went berserk. Around baseball roid rage is rumored to be the reason why Roger Clemens reacted so strangely in a 2000 World Series game when he caught half of Mike Piazza's broken bat and threw it at Piazza as he ran toward first base.

My experience has been just the opposite of what most people believe. From what I've seen, if there is such a thing as roid rage, it happens when you're on the juice, not after you've stopped using it. The most common psychological problem when people end a cycle is that they sometimes go into a serious depression. Personally, I've never experienced either great anger or unusual depression. I've always had a quick temper, but I was always able to control myself.

I've seen that kind of rage, though. One night I was with a friend who had a bad temper even when he was in a good mood. He was in the middle of a heavy cycle—he was definitely on the juice. We had just left the gym and were driving in New York City when somebody cut us off. It was the type of thing that happens every day, especially on the streets. Most people would get a little pissed, but they wouldn't do anything about it. My friend shouted something at the other driver, who responded by giving him the finger. As it turned out, it probably was not the best possible response.

About a minute later, both cars stopped at a traffic light. My friend jumped out of our car, and before I could stop him he had literally punched out the other car's driver-side window and begun pulling the driver out through it. I grabbed my friend from behind and basically wrestled him back into my car. Then I apologized to the guy. I told him I was sorry. "But maybe the next time you'd better think before you cut somebody off like that." The other driver knew he was wrong, and he was pretty shaken up. It took my friend a while to calm down.

I think the potential for rage is way overrated, but anyone who has watched baseball has seen a brawl. It's a very competitive game played for unbelievably high stakes. These are people working under staggering pressure, with their careers at stake. When I was working for the Mets, we knew that when a pitcher was taken out of the game everybody in the clubhouse should go hide in the trainer's room or someplace else out of the way. I can't tell you how many times I saw the door slam open, things get smashed, tables turned over, equipment get thrown. One pitcher walked in just as the phone began ringing; he picked up a bat and blasted that phone. This wasn't roid rage: it was the response of an incredibly competitive person who felt that he'd failed. I heard a story that in the late 1960s a Chicago Cubs player had to be tackled in their clubhouse as he was climbing the steps with a knife in his hand ready to go into manager Leon Durocher's office to attack him.

Problems like that happened a long time before steroids were available, so it's hard to attribute the fact that they are still happening now to steroids. But I have seen situations in which players have reacted completely out of proportion to the incident. I've seen players who would not normally charge the mound after they got hit by a pitch, or throw a bat or go after another player, suddenly erupt. There have also been unreported incidents in clubhouses where players have gone after a teammate for something really silly. And when I hear those stories, even I wonder if it had something to do with steroids.

But none of these potential side effects, none of the warnings about roid rage, prevented players from using steroids. Jack Armstrong, who pitched for the Reds, admitted that at least 30 percent of all players were using large doses of steroids by 1994 and a significant number of additional players were using lower doses to maintain. When pitcher Kenny Rogers saw a list of players known to have used them, he just about started laughing. There are hundreds of players missing from that list, he said. In 2002 Ken Caminiti guessed publicly that half of all major leaguers were using anabolics. Privately, a lot of people thought that number was low. My concern was making sure the players I was helping were doing it safely and getting the benefits.

As my reputation spread throughout major-league baseball, I began getting calls from players I didn't know personally. Truthfully, there were some players I dealt with that I didn't particularly like and others I never even met. Because I didn't run this as my business, I didn't depend on it to pay my bills, if a player I really didn't like or didn't trust approached me I'd completely avoid the subject. If he started to talk about juice, I'd turn the conversation to something else. There were some major leaguers who believed their own publicity, and as a result they just oozed arrogance. I usually tried to stay away from those people.

Probably the player I disliked the most was Mike Piazza. Maybe that was because the Mets brought him in to replace my close friend Todd Hundley, or maybe because he was just a nasty guy. He always had problems signing autographs for fans, for example. Truthfully, I have no idea if he used steroids, growth hormones, or any substance at all. During the investigation I was asked what

I knew about him, and I told them that I never dealt with him and didn't know anyone who ever sold anything to him. Piazza is one guy I would have been happy to give up; when I looked at his body, when I saw his disposition, he looked to me like someone who was on the juice, but that's my opinion only, and if he was using, I had absolutely no evidence about it. I am not accusing Piazza, just stating my opinion.

Once in a while, I supplied players I didn't like very much because they were recommended by people I liked a lot. That's the way my relationship started with Kevin Brown, who was a close friend of Paul Lo Duca's. I met Kevin Brown after he had signed his seven-year, $105 million contract, baseball's first $100 million contract. I could tell the size of his ego the first time I got his address, 105 Brown's Way. Well, that was the perfect address for him, because when we first met he believed everything had to be his way. Paul Lo Duca introduced us when he was with the Dodgers. Kevin Brown was very knowledgeable; I never asked him what substances he had been doing, but he made it obvious that he had experience. The first time we spoke, he spent as much time telling me how much he knew as asking me questions. I didn't like him very much, but that didn't stop me from speaking to him.

Brown was a very demanding, pushy guy, so right away we knocked heads. Basically, I thought he was an asshole, and the only reason I continued talking to him was because he was a friend of Lo Duca's. The first time we spoke, Brown told me all the supplements he was using, and when I told him he didn't need to use most of them, he made it clear he didn't want to hear it. Then Brown told me his whole workout routine, and I told him that he shouldn't be doing one of the exercises. "You're a pitcher," I told him. "You need to stay away from doing that. You're gonna hurt your back."

That's when he really got arrogant, saying dismissively, "Listen, I know what I'm doing. I've been doing it for a long time." And the unspoken end of that sentence was, "and it helped me get a $105 million contract."

"Okay, it's up to you," I said to him, "but I think you're going to have problems." I didn't care whether he continued doing them or not. What did I care about Kevin Brown? But his attitude clearly said to me: Who was I to be telling him what he should be doing? Which one of us had signed the $105 million contract? Finally, I said to him, "Hey, you fucking called me. I didn't call you. All I'm trying to do is help you. If you don't like it, all you got to do is hang up the phone."

Two months later he went on the disabled list with a neck injury. He called me back to tell me, "You were fucking right." I'm no genius; I didn't have any degrees, but what I did have was years of experience dealing with the physical problems that major-league players face every day. After that, though, Kevin Brown and I got along very well. We spoke frequently on the phone, for hours at a time, talking about the usual things: diets, training routines, and what to do or stay away from.

Brown was starting to break down. Steroids were no longer working for him, so he was ready to try the new best thing: human growth hormones, otherwise known as "growth" or HGH. He wanted to use growth for recovery. In many ways these hormones were more effective than steroids, but what was just as important: baseball couldn't test for them.

FIVE

Until about 2000 I supplied primarily anabolic steroids and nutritional supplements to players, but then human growth hormones began getting popular. The primary difference between steroids and growth hormones is that steroids actually build muscle while growth hormones promote recuperation. Human growth hormones help burn body fat while allowing your muscles to heal faster. The way I used to explain it to players was that when they were twelve years old, if they fell off a swing on Monday, by Wednesday the bruise was almost gone. But when they were twenty-five that same bruise would take a week or more to disappear because their body no longer healed as quickly. Growth hormones increased a player's healing ability. If a person of any age took growth hormones, that same bruise would disappear in a few days. It is an extraordinary Band-Aid for the body.

Athletes loved HGH because it meant they could do a hard workout on a daily basis—their bodies didn't need the normal time to recuperate and recover. Before safe, synthetic growth hormones became available in the late 1980s, taking growth was considered risky because the hormone itself was taken from the pituitary glands of cadavers and animals. Nobody knew what other substances they were taking along with the hormones. People who knew football legend Lyle Alzado claim that he was using gorilla hormones, which might be how he contracted the rare form of brain cancer that killed him. I never would have put that stuff in my body, and if anybody asked me about animal growth hormones, I warned them against taking them. Even after synthetic growth hormones were produced, they were much too expensive for most athletes because a cycle could cost as much as five thousand dollars. I knew about them, but I couldn't afford them. They were so expensive that the only way most people could afford them was to buy a small amount and mix it with the anabolics. But as the price came down, HGH became the next big thing at the gym, the next stage of evolution. A lot of people considered it the fountain of youth. It was incredibly helpful in reaching the ideal combination of physique and performance, and it seemed to be safer than steroids.

Here's how it works: everyone's body produces growth hormones naturally, but as a person gets older their body makes less and less of them. That's how your body ages. So, in essence, by taking HGH a person literally slows down the aging process. If someone stays on it long enough, their body heals more quickly, their immune system gets stronger, they sleep better, and the physical signs of aging will actually start to reverse. One of my clients was a plastic surgeon and we used to talk about it. He admitted to me that he took HGH himself and confided that if people really knew how well HGH worked it would eliminate a significant percentage of all plastic surgery. I've seen the results at the gym. Superficially, the drug tightens your skin, which makes you look younger and will even alter your facial features. For example, it will change the jaw line and remove wrinkles from the forehead. That's why plastic surgeons want to keep HGH a secret. When you take growth hormones every part of your body will grow. I've had friends who have taken it and told me that the most noticeable side effect was that their hat size changed because their skull had gotten larger. When I took it, the only change I noticed was that my shoe size grew from 9½ to 10.

Like all the other substances I knew about, I was introduced to HGH at the gym. There was a man with AIDS who started coming around. He was very quiet, a nice guy. I never even knew his name. When he first started coming to the gym, it looked like he had only a short time to live. He was very skinny, his skin had no color or tone to it, and his whole body seemed slack. But within a year his entire body seemed to rejuvenate. He had gained about thirty pounds, and it was clear to everyone at the gym that his immune system was successfully battling the disease. I talked about it with him, and he told me his doctor had him on steroids and growth hormones. That's when I really began to get interested in growth.

I tried HGH for the first time because I have a bad back. At that time I had three bulging disks and my spine was impinging on them, which meant that some days I was numb from the waist down, while at other times I was in constant pain. I couldn't even drive a car for a prolonged time without getting having to stop to get out and stretch. Like with most back injuries, I was going for treatment on a regular basis but nothing seemed to help. The consensus was that there didn't seem to be too much that could be done to help relieve my pain. My chiropractor was stretching me, I was getting steroid injections, but nothing really worked. When I asked my regular doctor about using HGH, he admitted that he didn't know anything about it and advised me not to use it. Eventually, I discussed it with my chiropractor. He didn't know anything either, but finally he agreed, "I'm not going to recommend it, but if it really does what you're telling me, it'll probably help." I bought a cycle from an AIDS patient at the gym. I had the chiropractor take my measurements before and after I took it—it actually made my spine grow three centimeters, which allowed the disks to float and, as a result, alleviated a considerable amount of the pain. Within five months I went from being in pain about 98 percent of the time to maybe 5 percent. Even my doctor was stunned by my improvement. At that point my purpose in using HGH was to get rid of my own pain. I may have thought about how valuable it could be to professional athletes, baseball players in particular, but I didn't immediately recommend it to anyone.

Most baseball fans don't really understand the way human growth hormones work. They are not a performance-enhancing drug. They don't build muscle like steroids. HGH certainly won't enable you to become a better ballplayer. While technically it is an anabolic, which only means that it builds up the body, the results from growth are very different from steroids. Inside your body HGH stimulates the production of natural growth factor, which causes your entire metabolism to speed up. That means, for example, that your tissue will repair itself much more rapidly than normal, which explains why a lot of doctors give HGH to burn victims and AIDS patients. There's no question that it works. The first major medical study, published in 1990, showed that when twelve men over sixty took HGH they had significant increases in their lean body mass and their bone minerals, which is exactly the opposite of what is supposed to happen as you get older. By that time it had already started to get its reputation as the miracle substance that makes people younger.

It's ironic, but it was the AIDS epidemic that made HGH affordable to athletes. After doctors began prescribing them to AIDS patients in the early 1980s, researchers successfully synthesized safe human growth hormones. At first doctors would prescribe four boxes a month for a patient who really only needed one or two. The patient's insurance would cover most of the cost, so the patient would sell the doses they didn't need on the black market to pay for other medicines they needed that weren't covered by insurance. It worked out for everybody. I knew bodybuilders who literally would wait outside a pharmacy waiting for AIDS patients to come out so they could buy whatever excess the AIDS patients were willing to sell. At the beginning, buying HGH that way was cheap, but then patients learned there was a secondary market for it, and the price went up.

As far as I know, I introduced growth to baseball. There probably were a few people taking it before I got involved, but not on any large scale. Like so many others, I thought it was a miracle substance. To me it was the perfect drug for major leaguers: it enabled them to play at the peak of their abilities every day without enhancing their performance. It eliminated the slight, nagging injuries that build up over an entire season and enhanced rapid healing for bigger injuries.

After baseball instituted its drug-testing program, it became equally important that—even today—there is no reliable test to detect the presence of growth hormones in a player's body. A player could take it forever, and unless somebody saw him, nobody would be able to prove he had taken it. I spoke with a scientist who has been working for years trying to find a way to detect HGH, and he told me that the only way he'd been able to come up with so far was to measure the circumference of the skull. As I mentioned, every part of your body grows and often a player's hat size gets larger. In fact even with all the publicity, even after everything that's happened, I guarantee you that there are players using it today. Major leaguers are some of the most competitive people in the world. If there is a substance that can't be detected and that will enable them to play longer or heal faster, they're going to try it—guaranteed.

Ballplayers loved growth. Suppose a pitcher strained his shoulder: typically he'd miss several weeks recovering from that injury. But if he took growth hormones there was a good chance he would be back on the mound a couple of weeks sooner. He'd be helping his team, earning his salary, and probably putting fans in the ballpark.

Baseball players definitely didn't use growth hormones as a performance-enhancing drug. My experience, which Senator Mitchell agreed with in his report, is that most of the time players only used growth when they were recovering from an injury or surgery. They wanted to speed up the healing process and get back on the field. Once they were healthy, all they would do is take small maintenance doses. In those moderate doses, HGH is very safe. The only real risk is that, since HGH makes everything in your body grow, if cancer cells are present they'll grow too. But because ballplayers are young, it's pretty safe to say that most of them are cancer free.

While growth hormones don't make players more talented, they can extend their careers. For example, Mets catcher Gary Carter had to retire because his knees were shot. If growth hormones had been available—and if he had agreed to use them—he might have been able to play for several more years.

I learned quite a bit about the advantages of growth hormones by watching their effects on catchers like Paul Lo Duca and my good friend Todd Hundley. It became obvious right away that it could be particularly beneficial for catchers, the players who take the worst beating on a game-to-game basis. In addition to wearing all that heavy protective equipment—even on boiling hot days—they're continually getting nicked by foul balls and pitches that bounce in the dirt and hit them, not to mention the collisions at home plate. Catching takes a huge toll on a player's knees because of all the flexing it requires. So if a player catches 150 games, it's just about impossible to be 100 percent for every game. That's why every year fans see catchers get off to a great start, but when it gets hot in July and August their numbers start to drop quickly. Growth hormones allow them to recuperate. That's one reason so many of my clients were catchers, including Hundley and Lo Duca.

A perfect example of a catcher benefiting from the use of growth hormones was Lo Duca, who was a good defensive catcher but not much of a hitter during his first few seasons. He was the Dodgers' back-up catcher when we met. Eventually, I started supplying him with HGH, which he used for recovery. But when he became the Dodgers' starting catcher in 2001, he surprised everybody by hitting .320 with a career-high twenty-five home runs. He also caught ninety-one more games that season than he had the year before. Of course I knew that Lo Duca had help. I doubt he could have kept his strength that whole year without the added stamina provided by growth hormones.

Pitcher Roger Clemens may well be the best example of the value of growth hormones to a player. My guess is that Clemens earned an extra hundred million dollars because he was willing to use substances. While growth hormones didn't make him a better player, they did enable him to continue competing at a top level of performance long after his career might have ended. In his prime Roger Clemens was one of the greatest pitchers in baseball history, but his career was pretty much done when the Red Sox released him in 1996. He'd had a losing record for three of his last four seasons in Boston. The next season, 1997, Clemens signed with Toronto as a free agent and had a 21–7 record, while leading the American League in wins, strikeouts, and earned-run average. This was one season after the Red Sox cut him loose. The following year he was 20–6. Who knew the fountain of youth was located in Canada?

Clemens pitched for a decade after the Red Sox let him go, and during that period he earned more money than he had made previously in his entire career. He brought hundreds of thousands of fans into the ballparks, helped the Yankees win pennants, and in doing so sold a fortune in Clemens merchandise for several teams. His ability to continue his career was worth several hundred million dollars—both to himself and baseball.

Roger Clemens was obviously a uniquely talented pitcher, but like every other human being after thirteen big-league seasons, his body had just worn down. So he did several things to slow down the clock. First, he started training. Clemens became a workout zealot and he got great results from that. Then he found that by using anabolics he could build muscle to restore some of the arm strength that he'd lost. And finally, when growth became available he discovered that could make the clock go even slower.

I know this is true because I supplied the growth that he used. The same growth that Roger, under oath, told a congressional committee his wife used to help get in shape for a *Sports Illustrated* photo shoot. I don't know Roger and I didn't see him use it, but I have no doubt that he used it himself. My good friend and a fellow trainer, Brian McNamee, had asked me to get growth for him. Brian didn't tell me who it was for, because we were both aware that HGH was illegal and we were careful never to talk to each other about our clients. But I knew Brian was working with Roger and Andy Pettitte, and I knew that Brian spent two weeks every month in Houston working with Roger specifically. When Brian ordered that kit, I was supposed to deliver it to him in New York, but I got stuck in traffic on the way to our meeting and missed him. "Just send it to me in Houston," he said. "Send it in my name, but in care of Roger. You have to put Roger's name on it."

I definitely sent it to him, with the package clearly labeled "C/O Roger Clemens." But years later when IRS agent Jeff Novitzky, who was running the entire investigation into steroid and growth hormone abuse in sports, asked me for a receipt for that package I couldn't find it. I knew that I sent it, I even remembered Clemens's address, but without the evidence my recollection had no value. I had a tracking number and confirmation, which I'd kept because

I'd written a note on the back, but no receipt. Believe me, it was unbelievably frustrating for me to watch Roger lie so smugly about Brian, a man I respected deeply, in those congressional hearings, knowing that somewhere I had proof but not being able to do anything about it.

But in July 2008, I found the evidence. I had to move a large television set in my bedroom. When I picked it up, I found an envelope under it in which I'd put receipts. I'd obviously hidden it there when I began to worry that the government was going to come after me and had then forgotten about it. I started going through the receipts, and there it was: "Brian McNamee, C/O Roger Clemens." I couldn't wait to call Novitzky. "Guess what I just found . . ."

For pitchers like Clemens, the big advantage of growth is that it reduces swelling while increasing blood flow. Throwing a baseball as hard as you can a hundred or more times every four or five days, for a starter, or as a reliever throwing as many as twenty or thirty pitches and warming up every other day, are definitely not natural things to do. Over a period of time there is a tremendous amount of wear and, unfortunately, tears. If you see a pitching motion in slow motion, it just looks like it hurts. After warming up and pitching in a game, a pitcher's arm and shoulder swell—that's why as soon as a pitcher gets into the clubhouse he puts large ice packs on his shoulder or his elbow, or both, for about a half hour to reduce the swelling. Growth hormones will help repair some of the damage and allow a pitcher to pitch again a few days later and be as strong as possible.

I experimented with a lot of different variations with pitchers, to figure out how growth hormones would be the most beneficial.

Pitchers obviously have different problems from position players, who have to be prepared to play every game. I had position players use HGH four days on and then one day off. But pitchers didn't need to be using it quite as often because they didn't throw every day. Going on and off would limit the most prevalent side effect, which is a numbing or tingling feeling in the arm, sort of a carpal tunnel feeling. Pitchers have to apply a different amount of pressure to the ball for each pitch; they need to be able to really feel the ball, so any numbness could have been a problem. I had several pitchers call me in the middle of the night soon after they'd begun taking HGH, telling me with real fear in their voice, "Oh fuck, Kirk, I don't have any feeling in my arm. What's going on?" Sometimes they assumed they had been sleeping on that arm, but more often they thought the growth was affecting their nerves.

"It's absolutely nothing," I'd explain. "Just get up and go take a piss, shake your arm to get the drug flowing, and it goes right away." Eventually, I figured out that it worked best for starting pitchers if they took it right after their start. So if they pitched Tuesday, they would take a shot Tuesday night and again on Wednesday, then stop. Two days on, three days off. They would get their next start Saturday and give themselves an injection Saturday night and then again Sunday morning. For relievers, it was most effective when they used growth for three days, then took three days off. After the first few years of feedback, I had it down to such a science that I could lay out a plan to fit every player's situation. I would tell them, "Follow my program and you'll have no problems. Do it your own way and you may have some problems."

When I met Kevin Brown, he'd already been pitching in the big leagues for more than a decade and, as I learned, had been using steroids. He'd thrown in more than twenty-five hundred innings, so his arm had taken a beating. But he was still an unbelievable competitor. Some players, after they get their money, lose the edge that made them a star. But he wasn't like that at all. His ego demanded that he continue to compete at the top level. He really hated the fact that he couldn't do the things he'd been able to do earlier in his career. That's why he got in touch with me. I remember him telling me, "Once I'm not able to pitch the way I want to, I'm going to retire."

Eventually, he became one of my clients. He claimed that the growth hormones definitely increased his velocity. He would buy six or seven kits at the same time, so he could have them available any time he needed them. I began working with him after he was injured in 2001. Eventually, he had back surgery and came back in 2003 to win fourteen games. After that, though, he thought he knew more than I did and went off on his own. That would happen frequently; I'd work with a player for a while, often while he was recovering from an operation or an injury, and then not hear from him again for several years.

When Brown was with the Dodgers, their management had a very good idea of what he was doing. In the team's postseason scouting assessments after the 2003 season, they noted, "Question what kind of medication he takes . . . More susceptible if you take meds to increase your muscles—doesn't increase the attachments . . . Steroids speculated by GM." Rather than reporting that speculation to baseball, the Dodgers just traded him to the Yankees.

When Brown got to New York in 2004, he called me and I began supplying him with growth once again. I worked with him that whole season and he won ten games, but there are only so many innings in an arm. Even growth can only hold back aging and damage for a few years. And after eighteen big-league seasons, his arm was worn beyond the ability of any substance to revitalize it. In his second season in New York, he just ran out of years and, as he had said he would, he retired.

I don't know if it's physically more difficult to be a starter or a reliever, but certainly the most difficult job for a reliever is being the closer. Some teams will use their closer fifty, sixty, even seventy times a season, sometimes in three games or more in a row. I don't think there is a more physically difficult job in baseball, including catching. Steroids may give a closer the extra stamina, but it's HGH that allows his arm to recuperate quickly so he can have his best stuff night after night. That's why there were so many relief pitchers named by Senator Mitchell.

Between 2002 and 2004, Eric Gagné was as good as any closer in baseball, appearing in 224 games, saving 152, and blowing only 6. What makes that even more impressive is that in 1997 he had Tommy John surgery, in which his arm was basically rebuilt. In 2003 he saved 55 consecutive games and was named the National League's Cy Young Award winner. I don't know what he did before Paul Lo Duca put us together, but I know that during the height of his career I supplied the growth to him.

Lo Duca was buying it for him, without telling me who the stuff was for. I didn't try to guess, since it could have been for any player on the Dodgers. And I didn't really need to know because growth hormones just aren't as potentially dangerous as steroids. The first time Paul asked me to send it to Gagné directly, he added, "Don't worry, he's used it before."

Gagné obviously knew what he was doing. When I testified in front of the grand jury I was asked, "What years did you deal with him?"

I shook my head. I had worked with so many players, it was impossible to remember exactly when I'd sent him kits. "You'll have to ask the government," I said. "They have all my papers." I guessed anyway. "Maybe 2003, 2004 . . ."

"Well, 2003 is the year he won the Cy Young Award."

I probably smiled. That made sense. I actually only spoke to Gagné once, and that was because he wanted to know how to get all the air out of a syringe. I explained it to him and that was it—we never said a word about what we were doing. Eventually, I did sent two shipments directly to Gagné, one to his home and the other to Dodger Stadium.

Just as with Kevin Brown, the Dodgers believed Gagné was probably taking "medication [so] that tendons and ligaments don't build up, just the muscle." Apparently, they didn't share these thoughts with the commissioner's office. It was to their benefit not to confirm their belief: the less they knew the happier everybody was. The last thing they wanted to do was lose their Cy Young Award–winning closer. That behavior was not just typical throughout baseball, it was the way they did business. That was the beauty of growth hormones: they were undetectable and nobody got hurt—and if they did, HGH helped them get better.

By the beginning of the 2005 season, Gagné was injured and never really recovered his stuff. I had stopped dealing with him by that time, and whatever he was doing, he wasn't doing it with me. But when the Red Sox were considering obtaining Gagné in 2006, their scout reported, accurately, "What made him a tenacious closer was the max effort plus stuff . . . [W]ithout the plus weapons and without steroid help probably creates a large risk in bounce back durability . . . ," meaning that if Gagné had stopped taking whatever substance he was on, it was doubtful that he would to be able to throw his best several nights in a row. Of course, that was an accurate appraisal. In the middle of the 2007 season, the Red Sox finally got Gagné to be their eighth-inning setup man, and while at times he was still an effective pitcher, the injuries and surgeries prevented him from ever again being the dominating pitcher he was.

Only so many miracles can come out of a bottle.

While players like Brown and Gagné knew how to use these substances, there were many more players I had to guide through every single step. Rondell White, for example, first called me in 2000 when he was with playing for the Cubs. I don't remember how he got my name. Rondell was one of the nicest people you're ever going to meet in baseball, and when I met him he knew absolutely nothing about steroids except that other players were using them and benefiting from them. He thought there was only one steroid and that everybody took the same thing. Like many players at that time, Rondell didn't know that there was a substantial difference between steroids and growth hormones. I had been supplying him with steroids for quite a while when he started asking me about HGH. He suffered a series of small injuries and had heard that growth would help him recover. He wanted to know everything about it. When he finally ordered a kit, I had to spend hours on the phone with him, teaching him how to take it.

Rondell understood it, but he was very nervous about doing it. Growth hormones come in two small bottles: one containing distilled water, the other a pill ground up into powder. As I explained to him, "When you take the cap off the bottle you'll see a plunger. Start with the bottle of distilled water. You put the needle into the plunger and turn the bottle upside down, and then draw back on the needle. The needle will fill up with water. Now take the cap off the other bottle, the bottle with the powder in it. Stick the needle into the plunger and slowly release the water into this bottle. Be careful not to shake this bottle and don't aim the water directly onto the pill. Shoot it on the side and let it mix itself. Initially, it's in a dormant state, but once it mixes it's alive.

"Then you take a second needle, a different needle . . ." I would supply needles with the stuff. I always kept a supply in my garage. "Put it in the plunger of the bottle with the mix, turn it upside down, and draw back until you've got as much in there as you'll need. Put the bottle down, draw back on it. There'll be some liquid and some air in the needle but don't worry about it. It doesn't matter. The shot is going subcutaneous, meaning right underneath the skin. Just pinch your skin and shoot it right into the muscle."

But each time I explained it, and I did so several times, Rondell said the same thing. "I don't understand."

So I went through it with him again, mixing and drawing and how to shoot the needle. But after I finished for the final time, Rondell asked me again, "So you go straight in with the needle?"

"No, you go in at a forty-five-degree or ninety-degree angle. You go underneath the skin."

"How far underneath the skin?"

"It can't go any deeper than a half inch, Rondell. Look how tiny the pins are." The reality is that with most drugs you can't put air into your vein or it can kill you. But when a drug is injected into a muscle, air will form scar tissue. I know people who can't shoot a needle into their ass because they've done so many shots that their buttocks are all scar tissue, too tough. But that wasn't a factor with Rondell. As I explained, and then explained again, "It doesn't matter. You're not going into a vein. You're shooting directly into fatty tissue or muscle. You can't hurt yourself."

"But what if . . ."

"Rondell," I said calmly, "if I have to fly down there, I'm not going to be too happy."

"That's all right," he said, "I'll find somebody." When he finally figured out how to do it, he became a pro at it.

Just like with steroids, I was always very careful to remind my clients that they had to follow my instructions about dosage of HGH exactly. I would warn them, "If you go crazy with the dosage, you're going to have problems. You see that with a lot of bodybuilders. They're ripped, but they're too big. Everything is growing; their foreheads, their feet, their hands. Some of these guys mix growth and steroids, and that's when they start growing muscle. Even when they sleep they're getting bigger. They can eat as much as ten thousand calories a day and still lose weight. You don't need to do anywhere near that much. Not only isn't it going to help you, it can hurt you. You take too much of it and you're going to make your heart grow. If your heart grows, it will cut ten years off your life. Just do exactly like I say and I promise you won't have a problem." I always asked my clients before they decided to use HGH if there was a history of cancer in their family. I warned them, "You need to be aware that growth hormones will make anything in your body grow. They reproduce themselves. So if you have cancer in your family you're susceptible. Growth can trigger things in your body. It could make a tumor grow. There's a chance this could bring cancer on faster."

In addition to those explanations, in my initial conversations with a player we'd go over many different things—and we'd go over them many different times. As I had learned a long time ago, baseball players are very repetitious. They often repeated what I said several times, to make certain they understood, which is typical. Everyday life in the major leagues is a routine: players follow the same schedule every day. They report to the ballpark at this time, batting practice at that time, and the games all start at ten after the hour. Players even eat and go to sleep at the same time every single day. Players needed to know how this was going to fit into their routines.

There was only one player who just could not follow my instructions and just couldn't get it right. It would have been funny if it wasn't so frustrating. Mo Vaughn was one of those people who, if you met him, you liked him. He was one of the most popular players in baseball. He was a big teddy bear, and after retiring from baseball he got involved in building low-income housing in the Bronx. But Mo was the most difficult client I ever dealt with. He just couldn't follow the directions I gave him.

I initially met Mo Vaughn in 1999 when he was with the Angels, but we didn't do any business. In 2001, when he was on the disabled list for the entire season because of an ankle injury that just wasn't healing quickly enough, he called me for suggestions. Another one my players, catcher Glenallen Hill, gave him my phone number. Mo Vaughn had tremendous natural talent, and since the game came easily to him, throughout his career he hadn't been forced to work quite as hard as many other players to succeed. So the problem was that when he was seriously injured, Mo didn't know how to deal with it. It was obvious to me that he didn't want suggestions about training and exercise; what he wanted was a bottle filled with a cure. He wanted to swallow something or inject something and be able to play again. He wanted to be playing. We talked about the effects of both anabolics and growth, but it was pretty obvious that steroids weren't going to work for him after he told me, "I'm afraid of big needles."

When a player was working with his own trainer, I really wanted that trainer to know exactly what was going on. I really wanted to ask about the trainer's regimen with the player. As it turned out, I knew Mo's trainer and I thought very highly of him. He told me that Mo had to be one of the easiest clients any trainer ever had, because Mo hated working out. He also didn't like to diet. That's a dangerous combination for an athlete. Mo was naturally a big man. Officially he was six foot one and his weight was listed at 260, but when he was injured I know he went over 300 pounds. Even if his ankle had healed, he couldn't play at that weight. His body couldn't possibly hold up. I had several conversations with him, and he decided he wanted to see if growth hormones would help his ankle heal any faster.

Mo didn't need to enhance his performance: he'd hit more than three hundred home runs and in 1995 had been the American League MVP. He was just desperate to get back on the field. For Mo it was all about recovery. I explained to him that growth would promote rapid healing and also help him keep his weight down.

I sat down with him in a hotel room when he came to visit New York during the winter, and we went through the whole process: how to inject HGH properly, what kind of schedule he should be on, what to watch out for, how to get the greatest benefits out of it, and what it would cost. He ended up buying three kits from me, including two less than three weeks apart. Mo listened carefully. I went through all the information several times. I was really clear with him. "Listen to me, Mo. You gotta follow these instructions carefully, particularly with growth. If you're not going to be serious about it, you're just wasting your time and my time."

"Yeah, okay, that's good. I got it."

"You're sure."

"I'm sure."

He was sure. That's what he told me. My mistake was that I thought he was actually listening. But then Mo proceeded to do whatever he wanted to do. He couldn't follow the routine at all and never worked out. When Mo went on the road, he would forget to take the kits with him. Or he'd take a kit with him and forget to take a shot, which is a problem because growth will spoil very quickly after it's been mixed. Or Mo would take it and not work out. Or he'd get the schedule wrong and just take it whenever he remembered.

I'd try to speak to Mo about it, but every time I tried to call him he had a new phone number. Even with his totally screwed-up schedule and his failure to follow my instructions, the growth actually helped him control his weight by curbing his appetite—although it didn't do much to help him heal. Finally, his trainer admitted we were wasting our time. That's when I told Mo I wouldn't send any more to him. He didn't seem to mind at all, and we stayed friendly.

Mo Vaughn was proof of the fact that these substances only work if you put in the work. He didn't do what he was supposed to do to get the effects he wanted, so the growth didn't work for him. The following season he was working out with an Olympic trainer trying to lose all that excess weight he'd gained while he was injured, and he blew out his knee. That was the end of his baseball career.

But Mo was the single exception. I know baseball's executives and owners vilify my name, but they ought to be on their hands and knees thanking me. It was me, and other people doing exactly the same thing, who enabled baseball to keep its stars on the field as often as physically possible.

After growth hormones became available and affordable, I rarely supplied just steroids to anyone, since players taking growth didn't need steroids. And when players found out that growth was undetectable, they didn't want to take steroids anymore. Sometimes, though, players wanted to mix them. Used together, steroids and growth hormones will make your body grow. You can build muscle, burn body fat, and recuperate quickly. Steroids and growth hormones make a potent combination—you literally could grow muscles while you sleep

From what I've read and heard about Barry Bonds, I would guess that is what he was doing. That's why it became so obvious when you looked at him—and that's also why he got the tremendous results he did. This definitely wasn't something I encouraged for my clients. Most of them didn't need it. They were using growth hormones primarily to recuperate. I warned them, "If you do steroids and growth together, you're going to end up looking like Popeye. And everybody'll know what you're doing."

Admittedly, I've tried combining them myself. I've taken steroids and growth hormones at the same time, and the result was unbelievable. I got up to 285 pounds with 3 percent body fat. I was shredded to the bone, meaning I had no body fat—and I wasn't even dieting. I just grew and grew and grew. It was almost as if I could look in the mirror and see myself growing. That's how fast it worked.

A question I ask myself—and doctors—repeatedly, and to which I've never received a satisfactory answer, is why has baseball made growth hormones an illegal substance? I understand why baseball has banned steroids, since they not only enhance performance but can be dangerous when used irresponsibly. But neither of those points is true about HGH. In fact the one substance that I have always believed poses more danger to players than either anabolic steroids or growth hormones is cortisone.

Steroids generally fall into two broad categories: anabolics, which build muscle; and catabolics, which break down muscle. Cortisone is a catabolic steroid. It's very effective at reducing inflammation, which can camouflage or eliminate pain. But disguising pain may not be such a good thing for a professional athlete. Pain is nature's way of letting a person know that they have an injury. The problem with cortisone and the other painkillers is that they reduce the pain without dealing with the cause of it. Cortisone doesn't cure anything; it just numbs the pain. It lets athletes play hurt. It allows injured players to get on the field. But every shot of cortisone damages the cartilage and all the muscle around it.

A lot of times the best cure for an injury is rest. Unfortunately, during the season rest is one luxury a professional athlete doesn't have. He just can't risk missing games if he can play. There's always somebody younger coming up who is trying to take away your position, and ultimately, your contract. In professional sports it seems like cortisone is the answer for every minor injury. Take a shot in the knee and go out there and play! We'll deal with the injury later. Don't worry about next week, worry about today's game. Playing with a slight injury can turn it into a more serious injury, sometimes making surgery necessary. Surgery means cutting away muscle.

So basically, teams were masking an injury enough that a player could pitch one more game or even finish the season. What can happen in those types of situations is that to compensate for an injury, a player changes his normal motions, the way he runs or the way he throws, or is forced to rely on other parts of his body. As a result, he is at risk of damaging or straining other muscles and, in fact, could injure another part of his body. Because of that, I've always believed growth is much safer.

Knowing that growth hormones promote healing while cortisone simply reduces pain, I continue to wonder why cortisone is so commonly used while HGH remains illegal. But if I had believed even for an instant that there was any danger in using anabolic steroids or growth hormones or, in fact, any of the substances I got for players, I never would have supplied them. I was just helping my friends stay in the game. I would never have done anything that might hurt them. Never.

SIX

I know some people still believe that I was running a major steroid and growth hormones distribution network. I think a lot of people believed that I spent most of my time conspiring with players to outsmart major-league baseball, manipulate the stats, and figure out how to break the most historic records by juicing players. In reality, what I did was much less glamorous. For me, what I did with baseball players was a minor part of my life. The reality of it meant spending hours on the phone explaining to grown men how to shoot a needle into their ass.

From the day I supplied steroids to Lenny Dykstra, all I wanted to do was to help out players I liked by sharing my knowledge. The way I looked at it, if my friends wanted these substances, it was easier for me to get them for them, and safer for them to use if I taught them how to do it. I didn't do it for the money. I used the small profits that I made to buy more product to keep on hand in case someone needed it or to buy the stuff I used myself. I wasn't trying to make enough money to buy a second home or a flashy sports car. I never intended to turn this into a business. But as my nickname, Murdoch, spread from Shea Stadium throughout the major and minor leagues, it became a business. Even if it never was as profitable as it might have seemed from the outside.

Players came to me because I had earned a reputation in the clubhouse as someone who could be trusted. I never talked. I never told anybody. Baseball has an active grapevine. When a player gets a good deal on a product, everybody is going to find out about it. If you want a suit tailored inexpensively, there's a guy for that. In each city there's a guy for whatever a player might want, and all the players know who it is. After I had advised several Mets on training and conditioning, I became the guy in New York who would answer just about any player's questions about training and conditioning—and eventually about steroids and growth hormones. Players around the league knew that when somebody needed advice about juicing, the guy to call was Murdoch.

Every player I ever dealt with came to *me*. That's important. Despite all the players I knew, I never solicited a single player. I never actively tried to recruit more clients. What I did, really, was answer the phone. If a player called me to talk about training or conditioning and didn't ask me about these substances, I never brought them up. There were several Mets players I really liked, and I was absolutely positive I could have helped them extend their careers, but I never mentioned a word to them. I would have loved to see reliever John Franco do well, for instance; like me, he was a New York City guy, and during spring training I spent a lot of time with him, but he never asked me about it so I never said a word.

I have absolutely no doubt that most of the Mets knew exactly what I was doing, they saw how big I'd gotten while I was working there, but only a couple of players ever discussed it with me. If a player asked me for help, I helped. If a player initiated a conversation, I would say, simply, "This is what I know. If you need information, I can help you."

When I was working for the Mets, what I did wasn't a business, it was as a favor for a few guys I liked. I didn't make any money on these deals, since I basically charged them whatever the steroids cost me. My only pay, if you want to even call it that, was a raise in the normal tips I got from the players I supplied. Whether people want to believe it or not, everything that happened to me started because I wanted to do a couple of favors for some friends.

Like everybody else who works in baseball, I got to know certain players very well, rooted for them, and eventually some of them became close friends. For example, Mets catcher Todd Hundley was a friend who became a client, and eventually a star. I think Todd may have been the first player I supplied with growth hormones. And his experience could make him the poster player for the benefits of combining steroids and growth.

Todd came up with the Mets in 1990. We are the same age, so Todd and I always had a lot in common: we liked the same music, we both loved to work out, we loved ice hockey, and his attitude about life and other people was similar to mine. I knew his wife and kids very well; I helped his kids with their homework, and when he needed things done in his house on Long Island, I'd go over and help him. Todd and his wife came to my wedding, even though he'd had surgery only a week before and his wife was pregnant with their fourth child. We were so close that my wife and his wife became friends.

All the clubhouse guys loved Todd. He was one of those people who didn't expect to be served; he'd pick up his own clothes from the floor, clean up after himself when he ate, and was generally considerate of other people.

One of the things we talked about was steroids. Todd asked me a lot of questions about them. He was very curious, but he was pretty clear about the fact that he didn't want to use them. He had talked about it with all the guys and had just decided it wasn't right for him. At that point every player was facing a similar decision. In 1994, when baseball was shut down by the players' strike, Todd only played ninety-one games. That winter he started wavering. "Maybe next year," Todd told me on the phone one day. "This winter I want to train hard; I want to get in good shape."

"Great," I replied. "But if you decide you want to go ahead, I'll write you a program." Todd had started working out hard in the Mets' new state-of-the-art weight room a year earlier. Once he started training he got hooked, so much so that he would even work out after playing nine innings. I saw how hard he worked, day after day. That was one of the reasons I laughed at people who believed that players like Todd, who loved the game and worked incredibly hard to improve, owed their success to drugs.

Despite all his efforts, 1995 turned out to be a bad season for Todd. He suffered a series of small injuries and played a little more than half of the games on the schedule. Even when he played he wasn't completely healthy. Todd knew those injuries were holding him back. Finally he told me, "Okay, I want to try anabolics. Can you put something together for me?"

"I'll walk you through the whole thing," I said. "Let me give you one cycle. Then we'll see from there." But I told him, "Don't be surprised if you see your home run numbers double; you're going to hit thirty, maybe even forty."

He laughed at me when I told him that. "I just want to stay on the field," he replied.

I'd seen Todd play a lot of games, so I knew that for him steroids could make a huge difference in his power numbers. He had what is known in baseball as "warning track power." He didn't have the power to hit four-hundred-foot home runs like Strawberry; instead he'd hit long fly balls off the fence for doubles, or drives that would be caught on the warning track just in front of the fence. I knew the additional strength he would gain from using steroids could translate into the extra few feet he needed to put the ball over the fence. Steroids may not turn line-drive hitters like Lenny Dykstra into power hitters, but they could turn a decent power hitter like Todd into a slugger. I set him up with the basics, Deca and testosterone. The benefits he got were immediate and obvious. He had a tremendous first half of the season because the balls that previously would have died on the warning track were now going over the wall by fifteen feet. What was funny for me was that even Todd had trouble accepting it. "It's just amazing how my career's taken off," he said. "The ball's jumping off my bat."

I explained to him that it wasn't all due to the steroids. "It's not just the drug. You're thinking that you're better; your body is driving itself. Some of it is the steroids, but most of it's your talent." Todd had only gained about fifteen pounds, which isn't a lot for a catcher. I knew that he sweat a lot, particularly with all the equipment he wore, so as soon as it got hot he started losing that extra weight. In past years he'd also lost weight, but that had been his regular body weight and with it went some of his stamina. The steroids gave him the extra strength he needed to play at the peak of his ability.

Todd had a fantastic season. He broke the major-league single-season record for home runs by a catcher, and the Mets home run record with forty-one. He was amazing to watch. I distinctly remember sitting in my house in July, watching a game on television. Todd hit an opposite-field home run with what looked like a checked swing and the announcer, I believe it was Ralph Kiner, said wonderingly, "Man, it didn't even look like he got any of that ball and it was way out of here." I smiled when I heard that. I knew exactly what was going on.

Todd was just incredulous at his results that year. At the end of the season I told him, "Now clean out. You don't take anything. You just train and you eat right." Then I set up a training schedule for him.

When I saw him in spring training, he was a complete convert, telling me, "During the season I want to do something."

I told him, "Okay, then we'll do it." I set him up and he responded by hitting thirty home runs. Maybe the most amazing thing about his performance during the 1997 season is that he was playing with a bad elbow. By the end of the season, his throwing arm was totally shot and he knew he had to have surgery. In late September he had ligament reconstruction, the Tommy John operation. When I saw him afterward, he knew exactly what he wanted. "I want to get back as fast as possible. They said it would be eighteen months. You think growth hormones will help me?"

At that time I wasn't supplying growth to anybody in baseball.

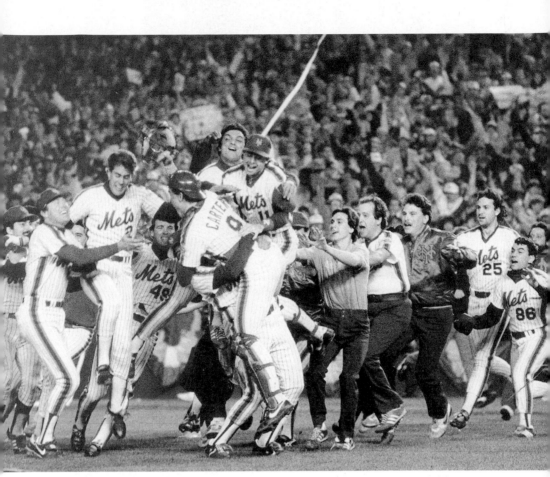

At sixteen years old, I was about to be at the top of the heap—as a clubhouse attendant for the 1986 world champion New York Mets. In this photo that appeared on the cover of *The Sporting News*, I'm fifth from the right as the celebration begins on the field. *Peter Travers*

The best part of working in the clubhouse was the relationships I formed with players. Here I am with pitcher Bob Ojeda at about four o'clock in the morning, after the Mets won the Series—and the celebration continued. *Kirk Radomski Collection*

After the championship parade up Broadway, we celebrated at City Hall with then–New York City mayor Ed Koch. That's me in the shadows on the right. This was just the beginning of my life in baseball. *Kirk Radomski Collection*

My friendships with baseball players eventually continued off the field. Here I am at Doc Gooden's bachelor party at a restaurant in Queens. Standing to my right is Doc's eighteen-year-old nephew, Gary Sheffield. *Kirk Radomski Collection*

When pitcher Roger McDowell didn't show up for the Mets' 1988 team picture, I stood in for him. I'm in the second row from the top, fourth from the right next to the then–first baseman Keith Hernandez, who now helps to announce Mets games on TV. When the official picture was released, though, McDowell's face was superimposed over mine. *UPI/Jack Balletti*

During the 1986 season, I occasionally filled in as a batboy. I didn't have my own uniform, so I borrowed one. I had just really started to get serious about weight training when this photo was taken. *Kirk Radomski Collection*

By 1994, training had become the center of my life. I weighed about 206 pounds when I competed and won my weight class in the Mr. Westchester contest, seen here. It seems pretty obvious why baseball players began asking me questions about training regimens. *Kirk Radomski Collection*

When the scandal erupted, most of the players I'd known conveniently forgot my name. Only fifteen-year veteran David Segui—seen here working out on a new piece of aerobic equipment he helped develop called the Real Runner— had the guts to admit the truth. Nobody loves the game more than David, and I believe he has been blackballed. *Mike Fish/ESPN.com*

My close friend Brian McNamee—training Roger Clemens above—was right with me at the center of the steroids scandal. Unlike Segui, Brian's client Clemens has tried to bury Brian, a decision that so far has badly backfired. *Walter Iooss Jr./Sports Illustrated/Getty Images*

Above: Generally the relationship between a felon and the men who pursue him is adversarial. But the men who worked my case were always professional and honest. I believe there is mutual respect between us. Leaving the courthouse in San Francisco are IRS agents Jeff Novitzky (left) and Erwin Rogers (center), and Assistant U.S. Attorney Matt Parrella, among other investigators.
Associated Press/Jeff Chiu

Left: I believe Senator George Mitchell, seen here with Commissioner Bud Selig in the background, was set up to whitewash baseball's problem. No one would cooperate with him—until I opened my mouth. The result was the Mitchell Report.
Associated Press/Mary Altaffer

I was guided through the most difficult time of my life by Long Island attorney John Reilly. Reilly's calm voice and wise advice helped me get through it.
Kirk Radomski Collection

But I had seen people in the gym recover from surgery much faster than expected by using HGH, so I knew how valuable it could be for that purpose. "Yeah," I told him. "They'll get you back in a year instead of it being that long."

This time there was no hesitation on Todd's part. "Let's try it." As soon as his surgery was over, he started taking the growth I had given him, carefully following my instructions. A little over a year later he was back on the field. But by then the Mets had acquired catcher Mike Piazza, and eventually Todd was traded to the Dodgers. Once Todd was healed, he stopped using growth hormones. The only time he used them after that was when he had another physical problem, this time with his knees.

Todd earned approximately $47 million during his career. I know I contributed three or four extra years and helped him increase his numbers, which certainly contributed to those contracts. During the investigation, I was asked by Novitzky how I felt when one of my clients, a player that I believed I had helped, signed one of those huge contracts that set him up for life. Todd, for example, signed a $23.5 million, four-year deal with the Cubs. The fact is that I was thrilled for him. If my friends do well, I'm happy. I can remember how excited he was when his agent told him about the offer. We talked about it. Todd's father, Randy, had played fourteen seasons in the big leagues, and the total amount of money he earned during his career didn't equal one-tenth of the four-year deal the Cubs wanted to give Todd. The new contract meant that Todd and his family were set for life no matter what happened with the rest of his career.

Although I never asked for anything extra and I didn't expect a bonus, several players sent me a nice check after they signed a big contract. I always felt good about helping guys. For me there was a great feeling of satisfaction in watching my clients perform well. For me it often was a test of my knowledge. It was like seeing a scientific experiment work out. It wasn't as simple as just putting the right kind of gas in the engine; rather, it was often a matter of selecting just the right blend. And as the players I helped had good seasons, the word about me spread around baseball.

In 1994 the Mets got David Segui from the Orioles. I took one look at David when he walked into the clubhouse, and I knew he was using steroids. From the look of his skin color and his overall body tone, I was pretty sure I even knew what substances he was using. It took David and me a while to become friendly, but he told me everything he was doing. And as it turned out, what he was doing was wrong. David is one of the smartest, hardest-working players I've ever met, and like a lot of people, he mistakenly thought that more was better.

David believed that the more he worked out the stronger he would get. I had to convince him that he had to take a few days off between workouts to let his muscles recover and build. Most people don't understand that. But David would actually reach a plateau— he would get the most possible gain out of his workout—and then he would continue training. As a result he'd go backward. Instead of building muscle, it would break down. I explained to him that physical training and bodybuilding were a science. I had to explain several times before he accepted it.

By working out together we became very close friends, and I began getting steroids for him. Eventually, I met his friends and former teammates. Ironically, when David began using steroids and growth hormones they were illegal, but eventually he discovered that his body had a physical deficiency and actually needed growth hormones. He was the only player I ever worked with who had a legal prescription for juice.

In the middle of the 1995 season, the Mets traded him to Montreal. That's probably when my hobby became a business. David played for seven different teams in his career, in addition to playing for Baltimore twice, and every time he played with a different team he would give my phone number to a few players. David would tell me, "Kirk, I'm going to give so-and-so your number." Then those people would eventually pass my number along to other players. My business really started to grow rapidly because of David.

For example, when David was with the Expos he gave my name to Frank Santangelo, who eventually became a friend and client. In 2001 Santangelo was with Oakland and he gave my number to Adam Piatt, so Adam and I developed a relationship. In addition to his own supply, Piatt bought several cycles from me that he later told the Mitchell investigation he gave to Miguel Tejada. When I sent the drugs to Piatt, however, I didn't know they were for Tejada, because Adam didn't tell me who they were for. With growth hormones it really didn't matter. Unlike steroids, there were no real safety issues. Small doses of growth couldn't really hurt anybody.

So each player told another player, who told another player—which is how my name got passed around to every major-league clubhouse—and through much of the minor leagues.

David Segui has admitted publicly that he took steroids and growth. He was asked once about his relationship with me, about why he recommended so many people to me. "The reason I became friends with Kirk was the same reason so many other players did," he replied. "Number one, he was a regular guy. He wasn't out to make a buck off players. He wasn't going to jeopardize anyone's health to make a few dollars. Believe me, there were people like that and they came around a lot. Players get to know who to depend on and who to stay away from. We knew he could be trusted.

"But probably what was most important was that he knew the entire fitness world. He trained people: he knew nutrition, he knew supplementation. So guys could go to him for advice about everything: What kind of protein should I take? How do you balance everything I'm using? What are the dosages of over-the-counter stuff? Kirk was the go-to guy for everything in this area."

That was the way my business began, and it just kept expanding. Certainly, one reason for that was that I treated every player who called me exactly the same way, whether it was Kevin Brown who had a hundred-million-dollar contract or a minor leaguer I'd never even heard of, named Howie Clark. When I was being interrogated by government investigators, they asked me about a specific player and I replied I didn't know him. "You don't think you know him," the investigator said. "But everyone knows who you are." I would supply one player on the Orioles and a few weeks later the team would start hitting the cork out of the ball, so I knew he was sharing it with his teammates. I've been asked so many times how many players I supplied. I always responded that I didn't know. Truthfully, I actually forgot a lot of the transactions. There were just so many, and it had become such a routine part of my life, that they all blended together.

I was brought up in the Bronx, so I'm a pretty direct person. When someone new called me, I gave it to them straight: "If you follow my program you're going to get results. If you don't do what I tell you, you'll get some benefits, but not everything possible." If I hadn't previously met a player, our first conversation—almost always on the phone—would be a kind of feeling-out process. Both of us knew exactly what we were doing, we knew what rules we were breaking, so there was an unspoken agreement that no one else would ever know we spoke.

During that first conversation, a player usually picked my brain to see how much knowledge I actually had. They would ask me basic questions, like "This isn't going to make me too big, is it? I don't want to get too enormous. I don't want to walk around full of muscle." Or, "What about those growth hormones? What do they do?" From their questions I usually could figure out how much experience they had with the subject. While some of the players I spoke with simply wanted advice and never ordered anything from me, most of these newbies eventually would say, "So if I was going to try this, what would you recommend for me?"

My response was always, "What do you want to accomplish? What are your expectations? I'll tell you if it's feasible or not." Their answer usually gave me a good idea of whether we were talking ana-bolics or growth hormones. Like the general public, a lot of players believed all steroids, including growth hormones, were essentially the same thing and had the same results. There were a lot of times I would have to explain the difference between the two substances. "It's like this: steroids build muscle and growth rebuilds your body. You won't get any stronger with growth hormones; you may actually grow a little more muscle or burn fat, but you're not gonna get stronger. In fact you may even get weaker from the growth because you're losing body mass; you are losing fat. But you aren't gonna believe how fast you recover from anything that happens. Trust me, the recovery is incredible, maybe ten times faster. Growth hormones will get you on the field and ready to play."

That promise definitely would attract their attention. And inevitably they would ask, sometimes shyly, "You think you could get some for me?"

But if we were discussing anabolics, before making any suggestions as to which steroid might be the proper one to take I would ask a lot of questions. "How well do you sleep? How much sleep do you need? Do you work out? Tell me what you do. Do you train after games? Do you go out after games?" I'd usually ask about any existing medical conditions I should know about, although with young athletes that generally was not a consideration. With black athletes in particular I would ask about hypertension, which is more common among African Americans.

Some guys weren't comfortable enough with me at the beginning to tell me that they already were using one of these substances. I understood that—they didn't know me. Instead the player would ask questions that tipped me off. For instance, a player would say to me, "If I can get my hands on this, would you recommend it?" Or, "If I could get this, how would I use it?" I knew the lingo, which questions meant a player was using already and just wanted some information. But as each player got to know me he would get specific. "I'm using test and Deca," he would say, for example. "You think that's what I should be doing?" Or, "What else do you recommend?" Or, "How frequently should I be taking this stuff?" "How long should I stay on it?" "What should I eat?" "Is there anything I can do that would help me more?" "Anything I need to watch out for?" "How much weight am I going to put on?" "Am I going to get sick from it?" "Is my blood pressure going to go up?" "When I come off am I going to lose everything?" "What are the long-term effects?"

The surprising thing was that in the thousands of conversations about steroids and HGH, with all the hundreds of players I spoke to, not one single player ever asked, "Is it safe?"

But the one question almost everyone eventually asked was, "I heard some people say that my balls are going to shrink. Is that true? Is it gonna prevent me from having kids?"

Once a player decided he wanted the substances I recommended, I sent him a package. I always sent all my packages by Express Mail, through the U.S. Postal Service, to their home, the ballpark, or to their hotel room—unless the player was going to be in New York, in which case I'd meet him somewhere and hand deliver it. I liked Express Mail because there was a post office not far from my home and I could pay by cash. FedEx and other private delivery services wanted their customers to pay by credit or debit card, and I wanted to avoid that. Besides, my local post office was inexpensive, easy, and convenient.

At the time I was aware that shipping controlled substances through the U.S. mail is a federal offense, and the government easily can get a warrant and open your packages. But I just never thought of myself as committing some kind of supercrime. I can't even begin to calculate the number of packages I mailed, but if the post office gave bonus points I certainly would have earned free stamps for the rest of my life. In all those years I never had a single package get lost or delivered to the wrong place.

Some of the players weren't quite as diligent as I was in tracking shipments. One time I sent Kevin Brown a package containing growth hormones and I didn't receive payment. I figured maybe my package hadn't arrived so I began calling him. A few days later he returned the call: "Everything's fine," he said, and explained that he'd sent eight thousand dollars in cash by overnight delivery to my house, although the return address on it was his agent's office.

"Well, I didn't get it," I said. I went outside and found the soaking wet package in the bushes. Kevin had checked the signature waiver box on the forms, and the envelope had been left in front of my house. Eight thousand dollars in cash sat on my front lawn for several days.

Only once did *I* receive a package of juice from a ballplayer. Jim Parque pitched in the big leagues for parts of five seasons. I think I supplied him with growth hormones two different times. But during the winter of 2003, he sent me a bottle of Winstrol that he'd bought somewhere and wanted me to check it out before he used it, to be sure it was okay. I knew the company, and I didn't like the way it ran its business. This was a company that introduced a great product to gain market share, but after that particular product got popular, it would change the mixture. I looked at the date and the lot number on the bottle and checked it in the notebook I kept. Unfortunately for Parque, it was garbage. "You can't use this crap," I told him, and I threw it out.

The price I charged depended completely on what I paid for the product. On most of my transactions I made a small profit, but I certainly didn't get rich. Whatever the stuff cost me, I'd add a few dollars. My cost fluctuated depending on supply and demand. Unlike recreational drugs, there isn't a locked-in price for these substances. The Colombians aren't bringing them in by the kilo. At times I could get a common steroid like testosterone for twelve dollars an ampule; other times it would cost me twenty dollars. For a kit of growth hormones, which consists of the bottle of distilled water and a bottle of powder—enough to last a ballplayer about a month and a bodybuilder a day—I would pay anywhere between eight hundred and sixteen hundred dollars, on occasion even higher. I charged sixteen hundred dollars a kit regardless of what I paid for it. Although when I could buy one for eight hundred dollars, I usually kept it for my own use or gave it to Brian McNamee to pass along to his clients.

Occasionally, I would send a package to a player and wouldn't charge him at all because I'd have stuff left over from another order or I'd gotten samples of new supplements or a product for free from a new company. If I wasn't 100 percent positive about what I had, I wouldn't sell it to anyone. I never had a single complaint, because I knew exactly what I was sending. That was one of the things that made players want to deal with me: I only got the best products available.

Whatever profit I made I would use to stock up on other products, so I had them on hand when someone asked for them. When Winstrol was available, for example, I'd buy whatever I could afford since a lot of ballplayers loved it. Or if, for example, a guy had five kits, I would buy all five, which would put me in the hole for several thousand dollars. But whatever it cost me, I never changed the price I charged. Some players would voluntarily pay me extra and include a tip.

There were players who would spend five thousand or ten thousand dollars in one order, which would be one or two cycles, depending on what substances they were using. Everybody's cycle was tailored to their needs and could range from four weeks to ten weeks.

I accepted all forms of payment except credit cards. My clients were mostly major-league players with good contracts, so they usually didn't have trouble paying me pretty quickly. There were only a few players I had to chase. And the only one who truly stiffed me was Jerry Hairston Jr., who still owes me two hundred dollars. The last time I sent Hairston a package, he said he was a little bit short and he'd catch me the next time, which never came. Jason Grimsley was terrible at math and would always pay me too much or too little, but he was a friend so we always got it right on the next order.

Players would pay me in cash, check, or money order. A lot of them preferred paying by money order because a postal money order can't be traced back to an individual. You just stood in line at the post office and bought it for whatever amount you needed and there was no record of it. Checks had to be signed. Those players who did pay by check wrote all kinds of fictitious explanations on them: most often on the bottom line the purpose of the check was explained as "supplies," "pants," or "suit." Some players would write "dues" or "GNC." The most creative explanation I ever saw, though, was from Rondell White. On the bottom of the check, he'd written "bought something."

Many players paid in cash. On a couple of occasions, for example, a player would cash a check with the concession department of their team. It was a lot better making the check out to the concessionaire than to a steroid dealer. One time, for example, Denny Neagle had a clubhouse attendant write a check to me out of the team's baseball account, which he then reimbursed. He just didn't want to put his name on a check made out to me.

I also worked with several players who really couldn't afford to buy these substances from me. A few of them I helped out by reducing the price or even giving it to them for free because we had become friends; especially Pete Rose Jr., who was a career minor leaguer.

As I mentioned, I had met his father, the should-be Hall of Famer Pete Rose, several times when I was working for the Mets. I knew Pete Jr., but I didn't really start talking to him about steroids and growth until he became friends with David Segui. Like so many other players, Pete Jr. originally got in touch with me because he had been hurt and was trying to get back on the field as quickly as possible. Eventually, we became very close friends and anytime he was in New York we would work out together. When he was playing for Newark in the independent leagues, he'd come up to the Bronx for dinner.

Pete Jr. was always straight with me. The first time we spoke about it, he said, "Look, everybody's doing steroids. I want to know everything I can about them." Unfortunately, he wasn't earning enough money to buy everything he wanted, so he'd only buy things every once in a while. When growth became available, Pete Jr. really wanted to try it. His problem was that unlike major leaguers Pete Jr. wasn't earning enough to pay for it. But it was so important to him that he played winter ball in order to afford it. When I could, I took money out of my own pocket for him. To this day he probably owes me three thousand dollars, if not more. I stopped counting. But if I had an extra kit lying around, I always gave it to him.

Pete's problem was that his body was breaking down; he had a bad back and bad knees. The steroids and growth helped, but they weren't enough. I know he never asked his father for financial help; that wasn't like him at all. I doubt he even told his father he was using the stuff. He loved his father but he was always his own man. I did ask Pete Jr. once if he thought his father would have tried growth if it had been available. He didn't even hesitate, responding, "If he thought it would help he would have tried it." But then he added, "But remember, back then none of this stuff was illegal."

Pete Jr. could play, but I think he got blackballed because of his father's problems. I know he never really got a fair shot. I think what happened is that teams just didn't want the problems that came along with his name. Pete Jr. was knocking on the big-league door but no team was willing to give him the opportunity he needed. To his credit, he never took it to heart; he just kept playing the game he loved. Having spent so much time around baseball, it amazes me how political a game based on statistics can be. There are career minor leaguers, like Pete Jr., who have the ability to play in the big leagues but for some reason just never get a fair try.

Pete Jr. was typical of the minor leaguers who had a major dilemma on their hands when it came to buying these substances; they knew that steroids might be able to help them reach the big leagues, but they couldn't afford them on a minor-league salary. Even so, a lot of minor leaguers took the gamble.

Word of my abilities spread to the minor leagues, and I began getting calls from young players who grew up knowing all about conditioning, weight training, and nutrition and didn't see anything wrong with using steroids and supplements. Getting to "the show," the baseball term for the major leagues, was the only thing that mattered. So a lot of these kids were willing to do anything to try to make their major-league dreams come true—even go broke.

Pitcher Dan Naulty, for example, was stuck in the minor leagues in 1993 when he began using steroids. Within months he was twenty pounds heavier and had gained five miles per hour on his fastball. Because of steroids, he claimed, he went "from an A-ball pitcher to a major-league prospect in two years."

Because they couldn't afford it, many minor leaguers would buy a little at a time from me, saving it until they had enough for a cycle. Or a player would buy half one month and I'd put the other half aside for when he was able to pay. If I'd gotten to know a player, or he was recommended by a friend, I'd send it to him knowing he would pay me when he could. No one ever stiffed me.

Outfielder Chad Allen was typical of the minor leaguers I helped. Allen played parts of seven seasons with four big-league teams, but he never really stuck. I met him through infielder Chris Donnels. He did anabolics mostly because he couldn't afford growth. For him it truly was better than nothing. After the 2005 season, like a lot of fringe major leaguers, he got a job playing in Japan.

Slowly, my business just kept growing. I don't know when it started getting out of my control. There was a time when it seemed like my phone never stopped ringing. Players would get confused about the time zone difference between coasts and call me after a game on the West Coast, at 3:00 a.m. New York time. I received calls in the movies, at wedding receptions, and even once when I was with my family at Disneyland. I was on one of the kids' rides when my phone rang. I knew who was calling and why, so I didn't answer it. What was I going to tell him, "I'll call you back—I'm on the Mad Hatter's Tea Cup"?

Often players would hit my beeper and leave the name of a hotel and room number. For security purposes most players don't register in hotels under their own names, so I had to know what alias each player used. I had spent enough time in major-league clubhouses not to be impressed with the fact that players were calling me.

Players did like to meet in person if it was possible. They usually had some questions they wanted to ask, and I always believed that spending time together helped build trust. So when they got to New York, as every big-league player did at least once a season, I'd deliver the product to their hotel or meet them for dinner in a restaurant. I only delivered a package by hand to one ballpark, and ironically it was Shea Stadium. I happened to have relief pitcher Mike Stanton's growth hormone kit with me when, coincidently, I had to go to Shea to drop off something else. I left my house, intending to stop at the post office and Express Mail the package to Stanton, when I realized he was at the same place I was heading. It occurred to me that I could save myself as much as six bucks! So I called him and told him to look for the package in his locker.

As my business grew, there were many players who I supplied

who I never even met in person. Relief pitcher Matt Herges, for example, got my number from his former Dodgers teammate Paul Lo Duca. Herges called me several times looking for growth, and over time I sent him three kits. Many clients were like Herges; after we'd spoken on the phone for a while it was pretty obvious that he'd taken substances before because he knew the correct way to use it and inject it, and knew what to expect. I didn't have to explain anything to him. There was just never a reason for us to meet, so we never did. If Herges used it as I recommended, when his arm felt fatigued, or if he simply took a shot every three or four days, each box could last him two or three months. In the off-season, I generally figured players would use a box a month.

Actually, there were a few players I never even spoke to directly. Gregg Zaun, for example, has been in the big leagues, mostly as a backup catcher, since 1995. I'm almost positive it was Jason Grimsley who called me in 2001 and asked me to send some Deca and twenty ampoules of Winstrol to Kansas City for his teammate Zaun. I got the package together and sent it to Zaun at the Royals' ballpark, and a week later I got a check from Zaun for five hundred dollars. This wasn't an everyday practice for me, but knowing Jason as well as I did, I knew that he would never supply steroids to someone who wasn't familiar with them.

Zaun was one of those players who later denied buying from me, but we both know he's lying about it. Zaun told investigators that he owed some money to Grimsley and gave him a signed blank check—and Grimsley filled in my name and sent it to me. That would have been a pretty amazing feat, considering the ink and the handwriting on the signature line and for the recipient of the check were exactly the same. And how many people just hand someone else a signed blank check? I don't know why Zaun felt it was necessary to deny reality. It didn't hurt his career: Gregg Zaun was never going to the Hall of Fame and baseball wasn't going to penalize him. Unfortunately, his behavior was typical of a lot of major leaguers.

Based on a comment made to me by Adam Piatt and Adam's later statements to Mitchell, I now believe Miguel Tejada also indirectly bought steroids from me, although I never actually spoke to Tejada either. According to Adam, Tejada was very careful to insulate himself from me, using instead the kits that I supplied to Adam. I had been dealing with Adam for more than two years and trusted him, so when Adam would call me back-to-back for cycles that we both knew he didn't need, I didn't ask why. But I knew all of it couldn't possibly be for him. Adam asked me to send him three cycles in 2003, but a month later he asked me to send him an additional cycle because "one of the guys wanted some." I never asked who the extra cycle was for; I understood the consequences and I respected the desire of players to maintain their privacy. I found out that Tejada was one of these "guys" at the end of one conversation, when Adam said casually, "I thank you and Miguel thanks you."

Tejada has forcefully denied ever using steroids—although there is substantial circumstantial evidence that he did. When questioned, Tejada claimed that he brought back injectable vitamin B-12, which is perfectly legal, from the Dominican Republic at the beginning of every season, and that's what he used. That's what he claimed, anyway. I didn't see him do steroids and the payments all came to me from Piatt, so I have no firsthand evidence. I just have my knowledge and my experience.

The most famous player I supplied without knowing was Roger Clemens. I put him in an entirely different category from anyone else, mostly because he betrayed my friend Brian McNamee.

I feel anger toward Roger Clemens because when he got caught, instead of being a man, he turned on Brian. Then he tried to blame his wife. To the last moment, Brian was trying to defend Roger; I know he lied to protect him. But in return, in front of a congressional committee, on national television, Roger didn't just throw Brian under the bus: he turned the bus around and tried to drive over him several times. He was willing to destroy Brian's reputation to try to save his own. Fortunately, it didn't work.

The irony is that Roger eventually would have been elected to the Hall of Fame if he had retired after his career wound down in 1996. But after playing another decade, after winning an additional 162 games—an entire season of games—he'll probably never get elected to the Hall in his lifetime.

Admittedly, I did send extra kits to players I trusted, knowing they were going to give them to someone whose identity I didn't know. I never once asked my friends who the extra kits were for. I knew that Adam Piatt and Brian McNamee, like Jason Grimsley, would never give kits to someone who didn't already know how to use the substances responsibly. I respected the desire of the players to maintain their privacy and understood completely why they didn't want to talk to someone they didn't know about a request that had pretty high consequences for their future.

I was always aware that what I was doing was against the law. But

I'd spent so many years saying yes to players' requests that it had become ingrained in my character. I believed completely that I was helping players, not hurting them. After all, I was helping them to get back onto the field, prolong their careers, and perform at their peak every single game. I couldn't think of a single person being hurt by what I was doing, so there was no reason not to continue doing it.

I never actually stopped to consider the consequences. To me, taking steroids or using growth hormones wasn't cheating. These guys were doing precisely what they were being paid large salaries to do: Be healthy enough to earn their paycheck by playing the game of baseball. Entertain the paying customers. They weren't robbing anybody, they weren't killing anybody—they were just trying to do their job to the best of their ability.

Conversely, just about everybody inside baseball knew that I was a reliable, trusted source for these substances—although no one knew the extent of my business. In fact to me the most surprising thing about the entire scandal was that so many people inside baseball knew what I was doing but for nearly a decade it remained secret.

One of the reasons for that was that my entire business consisted of me. The only partner I had was the United States Postal Service. I had no master plan. I wasn't BALCO, which was an entire laboratory set up to create designer supplements for players. I was one guy helping an occasional player on the side, first while I worked for the Mets and did other part-time jobs and later when I was a personal trainer. My office was my car, I didn't have assistants, and I kept most of my business in a couple of cabinets at home.

One important reason I was able to keep what I was doing quiet was because I never disclosed the names of any of the players I was working with to anyone else—especially other players. Inevitably, when a player performed some special feat on the field, which could be anything from hitting a mammoth home run to throwing a no-hitter, I'd get calls from other players asking casually, "Is this guy one of yours?" or "Do you know what that guy is taking?"

My answer to that question was always, always, "I don't discuss the people I know with anybody else. If I answered that question about somebody else, how secure are you gonna feel? If they want to tell you what they're doing, that's their business. But it isn't going to come from me."

I would always emphasize that, saying, "The only people who are gonna know we had this conversation are you and me, and, trust me, I'm not telling anybody. If you want to talk about it to somebody else, that's up to you. But I'm not going to." I think that response was reassuring. And I knew that in the clubhouse, using steroids and HGH wasn't a subject players liked to talk about.

Outside of baseball there was only one person that I confided in, a close friend named Steve Cohen. Nobody else, and I mean absolutely nobody else, knew even the slightest thing about it. And even Steve never knew the entire extent of it. I told Steve about it when I realized I might need a criminal attorney and I knew he could help me find someone I could trust. But otherwise nobody outside baseball knew what I was doing.

Many of the players that I worked with eventually signed multimillion-dollar contracts that set them up for life. So all I had to do was read the newspapers to know what my clients had gotten out of it. But after the IRS raided my house and I realized I was looking at a long prison term, I began to think about what I'd gotten out of my life over the last ten or fifteen years. I remember sitting at my kitchen table late one night, doing my monthly bills, and wondering if it really had been worth it. Financially, it definitely was not. One of the major misconceptions people have about my involvement in the scandal was that I'd made a fortune from my business. That could not possibly be more wrong.

In fact I suspect one of the things that surprised investigators was that I didn't have a large bank account, that I had no thick wad of cash stashed away. I didn't own big new cars or flashy jewelry or a mansion. I know that the IRS looked into my taxes and was surprised to discover that I had declared every penny. Among the many false claims made in the media was that I had built a big pool with the proceeds, which was completely untrue. If I had been doing this to make money, believe me, I could've made a fortune. The players trusted me. If I was doing this for money, I could have sold them piss: they would have bought it and paid whatever I asked for it.

What I did get in return from players—besides the payment— was anything I needed, especially tickets to games and events. In the big leagues tickets are a substitute for currency. Players are entitled to a certain number of tickets for each game, both at home and away. There was never a time when I couldn't get tickets for myself or my friends. I could call players for tickets for the All-Star Game, the World Series, and even events like the Super Bowl, Stanley Cup games, or concerts. Major-league players had access to all of that. My mother and brother are big Yankee fans, for example, so any time the Yankees were in the playoffs or World Series I had tickets for any game I wanted. When my cousins in California wanted to go to a Dodgers game, it required one phone call, telling one of my players, "Put them on the list, please." If I needed an autograph from a player for one of my clients or a piece of game-used equipment for a charity fundraiser, all I had to do was ask. From the time I began working for the Mets, I donated signed bats and baseballs for charity auctions, and even after Fred Wilpon tightened up on everything, players would still come through for me. The last charity event with which I got involved was for a paralyzed police officer. My friend Vinny Greco and I raised thousands of dollars from merchandise we got from players to help him. Whatever I needed, there was always somebody I could call who would help me out.

I've tried to live my life without regrets about the things I do, because I think all my actions through before I do them. And if for any reason I think I'm going to be regretful later, I don't do it. But truthfully, looking back on everything that happened, I really do regret even helping the first player.

I wish I had simply told Lenny Dykstra, "I can't help you," and walked away. Not for me personally, because I can live with the consequences of my actions, but rather because my business eventually caused so many problems for the people I love and care deeply about. I really don't care what other people think about me, but this certainly has hurt some of the most important people in my life, who had to become involved when my world exploded.

If I could go back in time to the early 1990s, I wouldn't have supplied one single player.

SEVEN

There's no way to accurately describe the way I felt the morning of December 15, 2005, as I watched Jeff Novitzky's team of IRS investigators sweep through my whole house, or as the government later described it, my "base of operations." But one thing I knew for sure was that my life had been changed forever. They searched every room, opening every closet, every cabinet, piling anything that might be evidence into cardboard boxes. There wasn't anything I could do but stay out of their way.

Eventually, the investigators carried out eighteen boxes. Those boxes contained all my financial records: every check, every bill, my tax records, credit card statements, and essentially anything else that had an account number on it. I had some anabolics and a few bottles of growth in the house at the time. I kept them in a bag in the top of a kitchen closet only I could reach and in a little attaché case in a bathroom in the basement. The investigators found everything and took it, including several boxes of pins, the needles that I'd kept on hand to send out with my shipments that were stored in the garage.

When they had finished their search, Novitzky asked, "Did we miss anything?" I wanted to laugh. Missed anything? These guys were total professionals. No one could have done a more thorough job than they did.

But I certainly wasn't going to tell them, "Actually, you missed some potential evidence against me." So I just said, "I don't know what you took."

Then Novitzky asked me, "Do you know Brian McNamee and who his clients are?"

I have some knowledge of investigative procedures, so from his questions I was trying to figure out exactly how much the government already knew. At that point I didn't have the slightest idea how serious the charges against me would be. Serious enough, I figured. I had seen at least one person who faced similar charges go to prison. I kept my answers absolutely truthful, but brief. "I know Brian," I said, admitting what I figured Jeff obviously already knew. In reality, Brian McNamee was a very close friend of mine. He was a personal trainer whose clients included Roger Clemens, Andy Pettitte, and infielder Chuck Knoblauch. "I delivered some stuff to him, but I don't know where it went from there." Technically, that was true. I didn't see Brian give the substances to anyone, although I had strong suspicions about where they went. But I didn't see any advantage in sharing that information.

Then Novitzky pulled out a folder from his briefcase and opened it. It was full of copies of my checks. It was pretty obvious that the government had already been through my bank accounts. He had copies of checks from Brian, as well as from players like Denny Neagle, David Segui, and Jerry Hairston. When Novitzky started asking me about these checks, I figured I better keep quiet. I told him, "I don't think I should say anything else until I speak to my lawyer." I knew that Barry Bonds's trainer, Greg Anderson, had spent more than a year in jail because he wouldn't answer questions in front of a grand jury, so I figured that the less I said at that moment the better for me.

"The prosecutor would like to meet you," Novitzky replied. Believe me, those are words I never expected and certainly never wanted to hear, but I was curious to meet the prosecutor and hear what he had to say. I didn't know at that time that Matt Parrella, who was prosecuting the San Francisco case against BALCO and Barry Bonds, had been waiting patiently outside in a car while Novitzky's team searched my house. I was driven to a nearby diner and the three of us—me, Matt Parrella, and Jeff Novitzky—sat down. Strangely, I remember ordering an egg omelet to be polite, and maybe to show them that I wasn't intimidated, but I definitely wasn't hungry. I picked at my food as Parrella began to talk.

"Okay," Parrella said, sitting across the table as if we just friends having breakfast, "everything stops now. If you sell anything to one more player, and we find out about it, you'll go to jail. If you take any drugs, we will lock you up. If you have an argument with your wife and the cops have come to your house, you're going to get arrested. So as of this moment, everything stops." Then he told me flatly, "You're going to work with us."

"Well," I said, "I need to talk to my lawyer. Let me talk to him, and we'll start from there." At that time I didn't even have a lawyer, although for a while I had suspected that this day might be coming. I figured that when the government announced the investigation of BALCO and Bonds, somewhere way down their list they would come across my name. In fact, about a month earlier, in preparation, I'd cleaned out my house. I'd thrown out cartons of receipts, telephone records and checks, getting rid of everything I could find that would associate me with the players. I'd kept only those papers that were absolutely necessary, and those were now in the eighteen boxes Novitzky's team had carried out.

For more than a decade I'd been leading two lives. I'd read stories about other people who had led a secret life, and they often ended with their deciding that they were relieved when their deception finally ended. Not me. I definitely wasn't happy about any of this. As soon the investigators let me, I called my friend Steve Cohen, the only person I'd told about my secret business. I knew Steve could recommend a good criminal lawyer. "Okay," I said, when I got in touch with him, "I think I'm going to need that lawyer now."

Steve called John Reilly, and I hired him that afternoon. Jeff Novitzky had asked me to meet with his investigative team at a hotel on Long Island the following morning. I didn't know what to do. Cooperate? Tell them to go fuck themselves? I sat down with Reilly to try to figure out where I stood. Basically, the first thing he asked me was, "Are you guilty?"

"I can't fight it," I admitted.

"Are there any smoking guns that can come out?"

"Oh yeah," I told him. I gave him the short version, telling him what I'd been doing, how long I'd been doing it, and with about how many players.

He was a realist too. "There isn't a defense," he said flatly.

After we had talked for a while, Reilly laid out my options. Basically, I didn't have any. "Here's the deal. I spoke with Jeff Novitzky this morning," he said. "It's okay to go meet him if you want to. The reality is that the government can bring multiple charges against you. I don't know precisely what you're facing yet, but it could potentially be a long time. They're talking about distribution and money laundering. If you want to fight them, we'll fight them, but it's going to be expensive. It could cost you a couple of million dollars, maybe even more." When Reilly paused I took a very deep breath. My future was not looking good. "But there's another option," he continued. "Novitzky and Parrella want you to work with them, they need you for information. They aren't going to charge you with anything right now." Reilly advised me to cooperate but warned me that if I did I had to tell them the whole truth. "You can't hold back anything," he said. "These guys are smart, you won't fool them."

At that point John Reilly and I had no idea exactly how much the investigators needed me. It was a huge choice for me to make, but I had been brought up to believe that you accepted the consequences for your own actions like a man: You didn't complain; you didn't blame anybody else. You kept your mouth shut and you absolutely didn't incriminate other people. The one big exception to that rule, though, was when those people betrayed you first.

When I met Novitzky the next day, it became obvious that I didn't really have a choice. The person who led them to me was an FBI informant. But I found out almost immediately that in order to protect their reputations, some of the ballplayers I had dealt with were burying me. From Novitzky's questions, I was able to get a pretty good idea of which players were talking. Usually when I spoke to someone, I dropped a little kernel of information that only that person and I knew. When it came back to me in a question, I knew the source. Did you talk to players by e-mail? I had only communicated with one player by e-mail. Did you send packages by this carrier or that carrier? Every question told me something, because each brought up specific events or circumstances that only one player would know. So gradually it became obvious that several players were cooperating with the government and had given me up.

I have to admit that it really bothered me. I had grown up with some of these players. Some of them had been guests at my wedding. I'd been protecting these guys since I was a teenager. I'd supplied them with steroids and growth—for their benefit. I'd risked my freedom and never made any substantial profit—and they were burying me? The players I'd helped and trusted were going to send me to jail?

I knew right away that potentially I was facing serious time. When I heard Reilly say "money laundering" I almost had a heart attack. I knew the sentence for that could be twenty-five years, and it didn't even count the distribution charges I could get.

It doesn't make sense to be the only stand-up guy in the room, especially when the people around are throwing dirt on you. Deciding to cooperate with the investigation went against everything that I'd done in my life and believed in, and it wasn't an easy thing for me to do. But I certainly wasn't going to take a fall for people who so easily ratted me out. Reilly had made it clear that the best, and really the only, option for me was to cooperate with the investigation and hope that the government went easy on me.

Neither Parrella nor Novitzky would make any guarantees.

When I asked Jeff Novitzky about it directly, he answered vaguely, "I can't promise you anything, but don't worry about it. If you cooperate with us, you'll be taken care of."

Reilly assured me that the government usually followed through with that kind of promise. "They won't put anything in writing," he explained, "but Novitzky's word is good because he knows that if he screws you over, they'll never get another person with a decent lawyer to cooperate." After thinking about it, I decided to meet with the investigators.

There were four people waiting for me in the hotel room the next morning, including Jeff Novitzky and Heather Young, an FBI agent. Any doubt I might have had that they considered me a drug pusher disappeared quickly. Their attitude at that first meeting made it pretty obvious to me that the government didn't see much difference between supplying major-league players with steroids and selling cocaine on the street. It was hard for me to listen as the investigators described exactly what they wanted me to do. From that morning on, I was supposed to record every phone conversation I had with a player. That was an incredibly difficult thing for me to do. It went against everything I'd grown up believing. There were actually a few times when I wasn't sure I could go through with it, and John Reilly would have to remind me what I faced if I didn't cooperate. "You really don't have a choice," he said. "You have a wife and a child. If you were single you could do whatever you want. But you have a responsibility to your family."

I accepted that, but if I was going to cooperate, I wanted to do things my way. I wasn't shy about telling that to the investigators when it was necessary. For example, when they told me I had to call ballplayers, I told them flat-out I wasn't going to do it. "That's not the way I work," I explained, "and I'm not going to do it now. I never called a single player to solicit. If a player calls me, I'll record the conversation, but I'm not calling nobody. They need to call me." I also told them that I wasn't going to entrap anybody. When a player called I wouldn't lead him into a conversation about drugs. That was the way I operated, I told them: I never discussed juice until the player brought it up. We butted heads for a while, but eventually the government agreed to those rules.

Jeff and his team gave me a tape recorder with a USB plug, so it could be connected to a computer, and showed me how to use it. We made a call to test the equipment. When they told me who to call, it was one of the people I suspected was working with them. There was at least a little satisfaction in learning I had been right. The rule of thumb is that the first person they make you call is working for them. As I dialed the phone, I realized that the person on the other end was probably recording his phone calls too, which I actually found pretty funny.

The first person I called wasn't a ballplayer, just a close friend of a ballplayer I knew well. He was a friend of a friend. As a favor to that player, I'd sent the guy one package about eight months earlier. I figured out later that the package I sent was probably the first evidence the government had against me. This person claimed he'd never received it, but I could confirm that the package had been delivered to the correct address because I had the tracking receipt. So when this person told me it hadn't arrived, I knew he was lying.

Actually, the whole situation was unusual from the start. I'd been friendly with the ballplayer who had referred him to me for a long time, but when that player came to New York for the last series of the season, he practically insisted that we get together. I found that request a little strange, because I'd been sending him goods for a while and he'd never made a big deal about meeting before. All of a sudden it was important to him that we got together? When the player showed up with this friend, I knew something strange was going on.

I picked up this friend at a Midtown hotel. I just had a feeling this guy was setting me up. So when I met this friend, instead of shaking his hand, I hugged him—and while I was doing that I patted him down to see if he was wearing a wire. I didn't feel any wire, but it turned out he was wearing one and I must have knocked something apart because it didn't function.

We went to a restaurant near Shea Stadium before the game, and throughout the whole meal he was asking me way too many questions about people like Bonds and Jason Giambi. Even though I kept telling him, "I never sold anything to those guys. I don't know them," a few minutes later he'd ask me about them again. It was obvious to me that he was trying to get me to admit to something that I knew I wasn't doing. In response, I basically I blew him off. We went to the Mets game and I left in the sixth inning. I didn't trust this guy at all.

Maybe I should have paid more attention to my instincts when he called me a couple of months later. "I need something," he said. "Can you help me out?" He was going to California for a meeting, he explained, and asked me to send the package to San Jose. I don't remember precisely, but I think it was two cycles of steroids and some needles. I had a bad feeling about it but sent it anyway. The address in San Jose was a setup—it was actually the address of an FBI agent. That package resulted in the only count of distribution the government was able to charge me with. When Reilly asked me later why I sent the package if I didn't feel right, I explained, "I knew I was already fucked." Now the government wanted me to call the friend and pretend like nothing was wrong. The package wasn't what it was supposed to be, but no one ever found out about that. "Did you get everything I sent?" I asked him.

"I got it," he said. I knew he was recording me. I wondered if he knew that I was recording him. We talked about the payment, which I knew was never coming. "And my friend thanks you," he said.

I hung up. It was done. I was officially a government informant.

I never actually wore a wire. I never had a recording device taped to my body. That's for the movies and the Mafia. Instead I just stuck a hearing piece in my ear and began recording every phone call. I think the government must have had the impression that I was running a drug supermarket, that my phone rang at all hours, every day, with players placing orders, saying things like, "Give me half a pound of Deca and a loaf of tes." At some times during the year, the phone did ring a lot, but December, when we got started, was one of the very slow months. So when my phone didn't ring through the whole month of December, Jeff Novitzky and his team got nervous. One day, when he was frustrated about the silence, prosecutor Matt Parrella told me flatly, "Okay, it's time. You have to start calling people."

"That's not the way I work," I said pretty firmly. "And I'm not going to do it. I already told you that I never called one player to solicit. Now, when they call me, I'll record the conversation, but I'm not calling anybody. You don't like it? Just go ahead and lock me the fuck up and I'll deal with my problems. It's bad enough I have to record people; I'm not going to entrap them." Even before the investigation started, the only players I ever called were people who had become friends, like Sid Fernandez, David Segui, or Larry Bigbie, and those were not business conversations. The last thing I wanted to do was get friends involved, so I refused to call anyone else, and the government finally agreed to that. So we waited for the first call.

Taping phone calls from players was probably the toughest thing I'd done in my life. In the beginning I had this idea that it wasn't going to be that hard. It wouldn't be fun, but I'd get it done. Instead, it was much worse than I could have ever imagined. Doing this went against everything I believed. It literally made me sick. I lived for months with this awful feeling in the pit of my stomach, a feeling that never went away. I spent all day, every day, hoping the phone wouldn't ring. When the phone would ring, I looked at the incoming number. If I recognized it, a horrible feeling just ripped right through me. From the day I started I didn't get one good night's sleep. I couldn't eat; in the first two months I lost thirty pounds.

John Reilly kept me going. "You don't know who else is talking to them," he reminded me. "The people you're recording could have already talked to these guys. They have too much information for it to be one or two players talking." He suggested that it was entirely possible that the person I was talking to was also taping the call. I still felt horrible every time I answered the phone, but I tried to keep in mind that the player on the other end could totally be screwing me for his own benefit.

It didn't help that, about two weeks after I'd taped the first few calls, Novitzky was pretty critical of the way I was talking on the recorded calls. He complained strongly that I was talking too much, that I wasn't letting the players talk. He really let me have it in a phone call, telling me, "You're not doing things right. I'm telling you, Kirk, you keep going like this you're gonna screw this whole thing up. You have to stop interrupting people . . ."

"I'm learning," I said just as strongly. "This is just the way I am." I didn't understand why he was so angry. As I found out much later, at that point Novitzky believed I was still trying to protect the players by cutting them off before they could really incriminate themselves. If that had been true, he would have had every right to be pissed—but it wasn't. It was just the way I talked to people.

When I still wasn't getting a lot of phone calls in January, Novitzky's team began to think that somehow the word had gotten out to players that I was cooperating. I kept telling them to stop worrying, explaining, "It's the holidays. When it gets close to spring training my phone is going to be ringing off the hook." After working with players for several years, I knew their pattern. I never got a lot of calls in the winter, but by mid-January players started getting ready for the season. At that point they would think about what they wanted to do during the season and stock up. And then about the beginning of August they'd start thinking about being ready for the playoffs, and the phone would start again. As I'd told them, that's exactly what happened. In the middle of January, my phone started ringing and didn't stop for two months. There were no calls from new clients, just all my regular clients. But it was a good beginning: over the next five months I recorded more than two hundred phone calls, every one of them logged in a notebook.

Every time the phone rang I died just a little bit more. As soon as a player asked me about obtaining an illegal drug, he had committed a crime and the government now had the evidence. My instructions from the government were that I was to tell everyone that I was dry, that there wasn't much around and I would get back to them as soon as I got something for them. I think everybody accepted that, because the reality was that I never knew what steroids were going to be available in what quantity at what time of the year. So during each phone call, I told the player to try me again in a few weeks.

I would keep the recordings I made and eventually hand them to a veteran undercover technician assigned to the investigation. Sometimes I'd meet this agent twice in the same week; other times it would be once every three weeks. Usually, I would meet him in Christopher Morley Park in Port Washington on Long Island. He had a whole laptop arrangement set up in the front of his Ford Explorer. We'd sit in the front seat and he'd plug the recorder into his computer and download the recordings. I'd have to stay there listening while he transferred conversations to his computer, copied whatever I had to three different CDs, put each of them in a different envelope, and then sealed and labeled them. To prove the CDs were actual copies of my recordings and had not been tampered with, I would have to sign the sealed envelopes. One envelope went to prosecutor Matt Parrella's office, a copy went to Novitzky, and the third copy was kept on file at the IRS. Sometimes it took a couple of hours to prepare the evidence, and I just had to sit there listening to myself talk.

On occasion we would meet in different government offices, for example One Federal Plaza in New York, but we always went through the same step-by-step procedure. Every once in a while I did have to remind myself what we were doing there: to me it seemed like a tremendous response to a pretty minor crime.

In addition to recording every conversation I had between December and May, Novitzky would call frequently to ask me very specific questions about particular players, trainers, pharmacies, even agents. It was pretty obvious to me that he was gathering information from various sources, although I was never really clear about what, specifically, he was looking for. Believe it or not, I was still hoping that somehow, somehow, I might be able to salvage my reputation.

But the government's investigation didn't end with me. Just like they'd trapped me by intercepting a package I'd sent, as part of my cooperation agreement the government used me to bring in other people. There were specific players that Novitzky wanted to force into cooperating with the investigation. I don't know why they picked those people, but when one of these players called, I was told to say that I was going to send them a package. Novitzky called these packages "controlled deliveries." The government prepared the package and then sent an agent to deliver it. The agent made sure he got the player to sign for the package, so the investigators had evidence. I think there were three or four controlled deliveries made to my clients.

I know that one of those packages went to relief pitcher Jason

Grimsley. I'd met him in 2000 when he was with the Yankees and had been dealing with him since. With Jason it was steroids, growth, and some diet pills. We had become friends, and he had introduced me to several other players. Jason was one of the few players who used to call me often just to talk, sometimes when he was driving, and we'd talk about everything except baseball.

Jason and I had more in common than the use of steroids: both of us had prevented a corked bat from being x-rayed. But Jason went a lot further to protect his teammates than I had. In 1994, during a game at Chicago's Comiskey Park, the umpires had confiscated one of Albert Belle's corked bats and locked it overnight in a storage room so it could be examined the next day. To save his teammate from being suspended, Jason crawled through the air-conditioning duct, dropped into the room, and replaced the corked bat with a regular one. Thanks to Jason, Belle's bat came up clean.

I hated sending the package to Jason, but for some reason Novitzky had focused in on him. The package was sent to him at his house in Scottsdale, Arizona, in April 2006. Having to call him to ask if he'd received the package was really tough. "You get it?" I asked.

"Yeah, it's here," he replied and, sadly, that was the last time we ever spoke. An hour after our brief conversation, federal agents knocked on his door. At first Jason talked to them, admitting that he'd used steroids, growth, amphetamines, and other substances and also telling them—according to newspaper reports—that "boatloads" of players using growth were getting it from the same dealer. Now, I wonder who that person might be?

Jason also told investigators that he stopped using everything except growth after baseball's testing program began. He agreed to cooperate until he spoke to his lawyer, whom I assume told him to keep quiet. The lawyer told reporters that the agents wanted Jason to wear a wire and to try to get other players to implicate Bonds. That probably was when Jason decided to stop cooperating, so the government got a search warrant; and on June 6, while he was getting ready for a game against the Phillies, thirteen agents from various federal agencies raided his house. Two days later, supposedly at Jason's request, the Arizona Diamondbacks released him. Less than a week after his career ended, major-league baseball suspended him for fifty games—if he ever played again.

I know three controlled deliveries were made: to Jason Grimsley, Larry Bigbie, and one other player. While the legal case against Jason hasn't been settled, Bigbie did decide to cooperate with Senator Mitchell and confirmed everything that I'd told them. Bigbie admitted to investigators that the only reason he switched from steroids to growth hormones was because he feared testing positive for steroids—and as I predicted he failed to get the same performance-enhancing benefits from HGH that he'd gotten from steroids.

The indictment of Jason Grimsley was the end of my active involvement. I had warned Jeff Novitzky that everybody in baseball knew that Jason and I were friends, so when his name got made public they would never speak to me again. That's exactly what happened. As soon as the raid was announced, my phone stopped ringing. I never got another phone call for help. Jeff told me he felt that the release of this information was necessary so that other players understood there were legal consequences to their actions. I also think he felt that they had gotten as much from my undercover work as they were going to get.

I remember sitting at my kitchen table, reading the Grimsley stories in the newspapers, and realizing that finally that part of my life was over. My phone had stopped ringing. I didn't really get sentimental about it, but after being part of baseball and dealing with players for more than two decades, it was impossible not to think about it, to think about all the players, the hassles, the results. Working with players had become part of the fabric of my life. Now someone had ripped out all the stitching. It was more than a little disorienting.

The one thing that made me feel a little bit better about taping the calls was that after the Jason Grimsley's name was made public, the only player I had dealt to who had the guts to call me was David Segui. I would have understood everyone avoiding me if they were facing prison or even a long suspension from baseball. But all these people, some of whom I had helped in a small way to earn a life-changing contract and others whom I'd known for years, just bailed on me. Only David was concerned enough to want to know how I was dealing with everything and if he could help. All the other players didn't know who I was anymore. They disappeared. I know what faults exist in my character, but that told me a lot about who these people are.

In late April 2007, almost a year after I'd stopped recording phone calls, Jeff Novitzky told me that he was going to make my part in the investigation public. Initially, the government wanted to announce my indictment during the opening week of baseball season. I guess investigators thought it was the perfect time to get the maximum amount of publicity. Unfortunately, my attorney wasn't available that week, so instead it was set for the last week of the month.

A few days before I left for San Francisco, where Novitzky's BALCO investigation was centered, and where they were going to indict me, in a very matter-of-fact manner I tried to prepare my neighbors and some business clients for what was about to happen. I told them, "In a few days I'm going to be in the news. I got indicted and I'm going to California. It may get a little crazy with the press, but don't worry. It isn't anything you should be concerned about. There are probably going to be some reporters coming around to make your lives miserable, and I'm sorry about that." My advice was, "If you tell them you've got no comment they'll go away. But if you start talking to them, I promise you that they won't leave you alone."

On Thursday, April 26, I testified in front of the grand jury that was investigating Barry Bonds and BALCO. Now it was my turn. Jeff Novitzky testified before me and laid out his entire case against me, but also told the grand jury about my cooperation. Then Matt Parrella led me through my testimony. Although Parrella asked me a lot of questions, I couldn't figure out where he was going with it. It didn't matter though, since the grand jurors had heard enough to indict me.

The next morning, Friday, April 27, I walked into the U.S. district court in San Francisco, along with Novitzky and Parrella, who stayed with me through the whole process. They told me what to say and how to word it. It was all a well-choreographed legal dance; in the morning I appeared in front of one judge and pled not guilty. After I'd made my plea, my indictment was unsealed.

The strategy was that I would go in front of a second judge two hours later and plead guilty. But as soon we walked out of the courtroom in the hallway, literally ninety seconds after my indictment was made public, Jeff Novitzky's cell phone began ringing and didn't stop. The press had gotten hold of the story. All his contacts in the media wanted to know what was going on. It finally got so irritating that he had to shut off his phone.

While we were standing there, I called one of my friends in New York and told him that the indictment had been unsealed. He got on his computer and Googled my name. "Nah," he said, "nothing's up here." We continued talking for about five minutes and suddenly I heard him say, "Holy shit."

"What?"

"You're not going to believe this, Kirk. You just got three hundred thousand hits on Google."

After waiting for two hours, I went in front of the second judge to plead guilty. I followed Novitzky and Parrella's instructions, telling the judge that I understood what I was being charged with and accepted the terms of my plea agreement with the government. My sentence was deferred. No promises of leniency of any kind were made. I was still a free man—but in the short time between the two court appearances I went from someone nobody had ever heard of to the notorious Kirk Radomski, drug dealer to baseball, details at eleven.

I went directly from the courthouse to the airport. To avoid the media, we had to wait in a completely different terminal until the very last minute before my plane was ready to take off. As I walked through that terminal, I glanced at the TV sets hanging in the waiting areas. On every screen I was the story. The whole thing was way out of control.

I couldn't wait to leave San Francisco—where I thought the story was so big because it involved the Giants' Barry Bonds and BALCO—and get back to the sanity of New York. I held out some hope that out on Long Island people would be able to keep this scandal in perspective.

But when I landed at JFK, another mob of reporters was waiting for me. A Port Authority cop I knew took me off the plane and got me into a private car. I had gotten my family out of our house, which turned out to be a smart thing to do, because the media had taken over my neighborhood, literally camped out in their broadcast trucks waiting for me to come home. I had seen the worst of the media when Doc Gooden and Straw had been in their sights, but this was even worse than I could possibly have imagined. I think most of my neighbors had figured I was exaggerating when I'd warned them, but to their great credit only one of them spoke to the reporters. And that was a guy I barely knew; but he thought he knew me well enough to tell a reporter that I had paid for my backyard swimming pool in cash, which was bullshit.

After the reporters finally realized that nobody was going to talk to them, they began chasing my family and close friends. And when all of them refused to talk, some reporters quoted people I didn't even know in their stories. For the next few weeks, I couldn't move two feet without the media following me. They tried everything to get me to say something or do something. Every time I left my house, a pack of cars would be trailing me. I didn't care, since I figured out how to lose them. Once I was on the highway and saw them right behind me; I slowed down until they got very close, then whipped a U-turn right on the highway and sped off. On a typical day, a pack of reporters would be waiting in the parking lot outside my office for me to show up.

I couldn't count the number of phone calls I was getting, both at home and at work, from just about every conceivable media outlet, begging for an interview. I would guess in the first couple of weeks I got as many as five hundred calls a day in both places. I tried changing my number, but the media got it within a few hours. The phone calls got so bad that one night I literally pulled my kitchen phone off the wall. It was endless. It never stopped, twenty-four hours a day. It really was like a feeding frenzy. I knew that these reporters were just doing their jobs, but I couldn't imagine what information I supposedly had that was important enough to generate this level of insanity.

In particular there was a real asshole from Fox News in New York who kept shouting at me, "How does it feel to be a rat?" and sticking his camera right in my face. If I hadn't been able to maintain my self-control, I would have smashed his camera—but then I realized that was exactly what he wanted me to do. This guy was an embarrassment to journalism—and in my opinion that's a very hard thing to accomplish.

Some of these lowlifes tried every trick to get me to talk. They would send beautiful, charming girls to my office to find out from my partner where I was. Reporters offered money to people who worked out at the same gym as I did to sneak in a camera and ask me some questions. A *60 Minutes* producer called my lawyer every Monday morning for a year to ask for an interview.

Most of the major TV news magazines called asking for an interview, some of them making it clear they'd be willing to pay for it.

Government agencies warned me that media outlets were offering a substantial amount of money to anyone who could record me talking about this case, and that I should watch out for people trying to get my voice on tape. So some of the tricks reporters tried were obvious: they would call my office to ask where the business was located—but they wouldn't even know what kind of work we did there. They just wanted to get my voice on tape. I would have new "customers" show up at my office to discuss business, and I wasn't to supposed to figure out it was a reporter carrying a hidden camera; but during the middle of the summer, when it was boiling hot, one new customer was wearing a suit and carrying a big bag. My business is now car detailing and preparing new cars to be delivered, and I've actually had reporters show up at the front door, supposedly to talk business, without a car. Some must have thought I was an idiot.

After weeks of this absurdity, I realized that the media was so intent on beating each other to the story that they had lost sight of what the story was—I was a guy who had sold steroids and hormones to major-league baseball players. The more I avoided them the more they wanted me. I knew it wasn't me they were really interested in; the only thing they wanted from me was an admission that I'd sold drugs to the biggest stars in baseball. They wanted me to name the biggest names. They weren't interested in a legitimate story; they wanted a scandal! They wanted readers and ratings. If a reporter could somehow convince me to name stars who were juicing, they could turn the story into a major scandal and guarantee tremendous publicity for themselves.

Almost every reporter told me I should use their outlet "to get your story out. Set the record straight." They all told me exactly the same thing: "I'm not like all the other reporters. Believe me, I'm the only one you can trust." A *New York Post* reporter told me, "I just want to know what you're feeling about all this. I won't print anything."

I told him, "Listen, legally I can't comment on anything. I'm just glad it's done."

The next day that same reporter wrote a half-page article quoting me as saying things I never said. They wanted to take me out for lunch, get to know me, prove to me that their only concern was getting the story right. Meanwhile, there was a helicopter circling my house waiting for me to come out. The only reporter I spoke with was Mike Fish of ESPN, who quoted me precisely and then went over his story with me for accuracy, as he had agreed to do, before it was printed.

There were so many lies written about me. Anyone who read the newspapers or watched news reports probably believed that I was a major drug dealer. According to the papers, the IRS found hundreds of thousands of doses in my house—which would have been amazing considering I kept everything in one cabinet and a pouch intended to hold shaving equipment. But according to the media, I had a lab in my house, a house that I had paid for from the money I made. The reporters made me sound like I was just another big-league hanger-on, a jock sniffer preying on the players and turning them into drug users to make money. They made it seem like

I had single-handedly destroyed the integrity of the game. What was reported, with the exception of Fish's story, couldn't have been further from the truth.

I shouldn't have been surprised. When I was working for the Mets, I saw how some reporters make up stories about players. There were nights when I went out with a player and knew everything that went on, but a few days later I'd read a completely fictitious story about what had happened. Although I was smart enough to keep away from those reporters, I have to admit that before I was in the middle of it I really had no idea how crazy it could get. For months, they tracked every move I made.

But what the press did to me was nothing compared to the way the Mets organization tried to betray me. I was told by someone in the government that the Mets organization was going to try to discredit me.

I'd done everything possible to protect the Mets from being associated with me. It wasn't the organization's fault that I did what I did. I made sure that the plea agreement I signed with the government stated very clearly that I didn't work for the Mets when I was distributing steroids and growth hormones. The agreement stated that I began doing this in 1995, the year I left the Mets. I asked for that date because I didn't want this scandal to affect the good people I'd worked with who were still with the Mets. The government agreed to that—even though I had actually started distributing during the last few seasons that I was working at Shea.

When I heard from my sources that the Mets were getting ready to disown me, I got angry. I called my old boss and told him forcefully that I wasn't fooling around. "Listen, I heard that the Mets are going to try to discredit me. I advise you to tell whomever you have to tell that if they start a smear campaign I'm going to open up a can of worms that's not going to make them happy. I've got plenty of crap that I never said one word about. So you tell them not to ruffle my feathers. If they want to play this game, I will win."

After that, the only thing the Mets tried to do was downplay the years I worked there.

I spent a lot of the next year wondering if I was going to prison. Since I had no idea what my future was going to be, my life had to be completely on hold. It was impossible for me to do anything more than make basic decisions. Usually, when you make a plea agreement for a crime that is handled in a local or state court, your lawyer can make a deal with the judge. But in federal court, the judge has the right to make any decision he or she wants in regard to sentencing. Until that decision comes out of his or her mouth, nobody knows what it's going to be. The prosecutor can make recommendations, but the judge can choose to ignore it and hand out whatever sentence he or she wants to impose. Throughout the sentencing process, Jeff Novitzky and Matt Parrella tried to be reassuring, but it didn't help because we all knew the judge was going to do whatever he or she wanted. Novitzky told me several times, "I can't promise you anything, but don't worry about it." In fact when Novitzky and Parrella had interviewed David Segui, David had asked them what my sentence would be. Jeff told him flatly, "He'll get probation."

When David told me what Novitzky had said, I replied, "That's great, but I got nothing in writing." When it's your ass on the line, predictions don't have a whole lot of meaning. The government had given me what is called a 5K1.1 letter, a very unusual and important piece of paper. It's basically a statement from the government verifying that an individual has provided valuable assistance in an investigation and that cooperation should be considered and rewarded by the judge when deciding on a sentence. John Reilly told me that he had clients who had given up murderers and couldn't get a 5K1.1 letter, so he was surprised and very pleased when Novitzky and Parrella offered one to me without even being asked.

The government had postponed my sentencing three different times, which I was pretty sure was intended to keep me under control. Until I was sentenced, I couldn't speak to anyone about the case, which was the way I thought the government wanted it. During this time, as I later I found out, there were some pretty tough negotiations taking place among Novitzky, Parrella, and other government officials. A couple of officials really wanted me to serve time, even just three to six months, in order to show people that the government was going to be tough in cases like mine. But Novitzky and Parrella argued against that because the message they wanted to communicate to the public was that good things happen if you cooperate with a government investigation.

As John Reilly pointed out to me, if I went to jail, even for a short period of time, no lawyer in the future would ever allow a client to cooperate with the government unless there was a written promise of lenient treatment. I was pretty angry that I was left hanging; I'd fulfilled every paragraph of my plea agreement. So I told Reilly that if I got even one day of jail time, "I'll scream so loud that every lawyer in America demands a guaranteed agreement in writing before their client agrees to cooperate."

I really just wanted everything to be over with. The waiting and not knowing had made it the longest period of my life. I tried hard not to show the strain, but there were a lot of times I wished it was all a dream and I would wake up and go on with my real life. I needed to know what my future was going to be.

Finally, I got a date for sentencing: February 7, 2008. I returned to San Francisco the day before, and I remember sitting on the airplane, very nervous about my future. I'd bought a return ticket, but I didn't know if I'd get to use it. Jeff Novitzky stayed with me the entire time, from picking me up at the airport to preparing me for each step. I'd done so many different things in my life, but I'd never before stood in front of a judge, waiting to hear my fate. That was terrifying. As much faith as I had in my lawyer and the agents, I knew my life was really in the hands of the judge.

The next morning the investigators brought me into the courthouse through an underground garage so we didn't have to face the media. Five minutes before my case was scheduled to be called, we pushed our way through a pack of reporters and went into the courtroom. When my sentencing began, Matt Parrella told Judge Susan Illston that I had been "the most significant cooperator in the arena of sports [steroid investigation] to date. His extensive and immediate cooperation deserves recognition." It almost sounded like my high school graduation rather than a prosecutor speaking at my sentencing. But finally, Parrella concluded by saying that because of my unprecedented level of cooperation the government was asking the judge to grant me probation.

Next it was my turn. I stood up and faced Judge Illston. "I take full responsibility," I said, and apologized to the court. I meant every single word I said. What had started as a favor for a couple of players had become front-page news and could cause me to lose my freedom. You bet I was sorry.

When I finished, Judge Illston began sentencing me. At first it did not go as I had expected. "I want you to understand," she said sternly, looking straight at me, "I view these as very serious offenses." Then she began to lecture me about the damage that I'd done specifically to the game of baseball and by extension to society. She pointed out that young people look up to baseball players as role models and that, by enabling them to cheat, together we had sent a horrible message to those kids.

As I listened to her I was thinking, oh shit, she's going to put me in jail. My heart dropped—I was going to prison. I looked at John Reilly, but it was obvious he didn't know what to do. I glanced at Jeff, who seemed as surprised as I was. But then the lecture ended and she sentenced me to five years probation and an $18,575 fine. "This is not a free lunch," Judge Illston said, and warned me that if I didn't continue to cooperate I'd be standing in front of her again and that the outcome would be very different. I was going to be very closely supervised, she said, and nothing less than perfect behavior was going to be acceptable.

I listened carefully, but I was elated. I was going home. When we were finished, Jeff took me out of the courthouse and drove me back to the hotel. While we were in the car he said, "I told you everything would work out," although he admitted that when the judge started reprimanding me, "I got nervous there for a second. That wasn't the way I expected it to go."

Although Jeff and I had our disagreements, especially at the beginning, we had gotten to know each other since that early morning when he'd knocked on my door. I respected him. "You did your job and I accept that," I told him. "I appreciate everything you did for me."

As much as it is possible to become friends with someone who is prosecuting you, I like to believe that Jeff and I became friends. My relationship with Jeff Novitzky was one of the most unusual of my life. Jeff is a completely bald, six-foot-six, no-nonsense government cop who sticks out in every crowd. He's everybody's nightmare: a really smart, diligent IRS agent. Jeff didn't get lucky on this investigation: he is an unbelievably thorough investigator and a very fair guy. I will always admire him for his professionalism; he could have treated me like a felon, but he didn't. He always treated me with dignity. It was never personal with him; it was always doing the right thing for the job. And I respected him for that.

For a long time Jeff held my fate in his hands. You learn everything you need to know about a person by watching how they exercise the power they hold over other people. Jeff never abused his position, but actually tried to make this situation as tolerable as possible for me. We have stayed in contact. After the sentencing he continued to call me, a lot of times to ask questions about the cases he was working on, but sometimes just to see how I was doing. In the summer of '08 he was promoted to a position with the Federal Drug Administration, where he's going to go after supplement companies that push their products at young people.

Just because I didn't go to prison doesn't mean that I got off light. I was definitely punished. I'm a convicted felon, which carries a lot of penalties. I can't vote, for example. I can't ever coach kids. As long as I'm on probation, at least five years from the day I was sentenced, I can't leave the country without permission; I have to make a formal request six months in advance and the government can turn me down for any reason. I've already been told which countries to forget about visiting. Every month I have to provide an itemized statement of every penny I earn and spend. If I take more than a thousand dollars out of the bank, I have to tell the government where it's going, and if I buy something for more than five hundred dollars I have to report it. The government can search my house or my cars at any time, for any reason. I'm continually tested for drugs. Basically, the government owns my life while on I'm probation.

Because of the money-laundering charge, it's very difficult for me to do anything with banks. Baseball took its revenge too: I was out to dinner with my family in Rockefeller Center two weeks before Christmas. When I paid with a Chase Visa card, it was declined. I gave them a second card: also declined. That didn't make sense, since I had perfect credit and never had a problem. I called Chase and the person I spoke with wouldn't give me an explanation. But when my wife called someone told her, "It has to do with the primary cardholder." Me. A week later I got a letter explaining that my credit cards had been canceled for "inconsistent activities." I called an investigator at the IRS, who told me that someone in baseball had informed the bank who I was. It turned out that Chase is a corporate sponsor of baseball. So as a convicted felon, I have difficulty getting credit from Chase and other banks.

That doesn't even include the fine. Now, $18,575 doesn't seem like a lot of money—until it's you that has to pay it. So I've been paying that off every month.

Maybe above all else, the worst punishment is the notoriety. No matter what I do for the rest of my life, no matter how I live or what good I do for my community or for other people, the only thing about me that people will ever know is that I'm the guy who provided steroids to baseball.

EIGHT

Baseball had set up Senator George Mitchell to fail. After the BALCO scandal; the continuing speculation about Barry Bonds's steroid use; the admission by Jason Giambi that he had used juice; the questions about players like Mark McGwire; the 2005 congressional hearings in which everybody denied everything; and the growing number of big stars, including Miguel Tejada and Sammy Sosa, who had become suspect, the public was really wondering about the extent of performance-enhancing substance use in baseball. So Commissioner Bud Selig decided that baseball had to conduct its own private investigation into the use of steroids and growth hormones. To lead that investigation they hired one of the most respected men in the country, Senator George Mitchell, whose integrity couldn't be questioned.

After they hired him, though, baseball did everything possible to make sure he wouldn't prove anything. Because this was a private investigation, Senator Mitchell had no subpoena power, he couldn't force anyone to answer his questions, and the Players Association, the union of major-league players, practically prohibited its members from cooperating with him.

The Mitchell Report was supposed to be a whitewash: I believe its planned purpose was to allow baseball to hide behind George Mitchell's reputation. Why would club owners hurt their own business? They knew the investigation was going to fail. When Senator Mitchell finally issued what would have to be a very general and inconclusive report because no one would talk to him, baseball could claim that a long investigation—by an accomplished, trustworthy former senator—had shown that the game was relatively free of performance-enhancing drugs. The report would state that whatever problems with steroids there had been in baseball, they were isolated or already dealt with. The report would be the perfect solution to a widespread problem.

Baseball didn't plan on me getting involved.

Of course I never set out to cooperate either. Unfortunately, like so many other things, it wasn't my choice. If the government hadn't forced me to do it, I would never have agreed to meet Senator Mitchell. In fact about two weeks after baseball announced the Mitchell investigation, Brian McNamee and I were in a car and he asked me what I would do if Mitchell called me. "You kidding?" I said. "I'd tell him to go fuck himself. I would never talk to him. Why would I talk to him? He's working for baseball, for the owners. I don't need to say anything to him."

But about two weeks after I was arrested, Jeff Novitzky told me that as part of my plea agreement, "You have to sit down with Senator Mitchell." I was being given immunity, he said, meaning nothing I told Mitchell's investigators could be used to prosecute me, but I had to answer all of his questions and treat the whole thing like I was talking to Novitzky and his team. Obviously, I wasn't happy about it, but by this point I had signed a cooperation agreement, I had given my word, and when I do that I always follow through.

Jeff Novitzky had given me a little background about Senator Mitchell, but the day before my first meeting with him I Googled his name. Until I did my own research, I hadn't really understood why baseball had picked him specifically to conduct this investigation. George Mitchell had served in the United States Senate for fifteen years, eventually being elected the Democratic majority leader. After turning down an offer from President Clinton to be appointed to the United States Supreme Court, he helped negotiate the treaty that brought peace to Northern Ireland. After retiring from politics, he had practiced law in New York and become the chairman of the Walt Disney Company. He was a very impressive guy, and I think it's fair to say that we were an unlikely team. I did as much homework on Mitchell as I could on the Internet. Apparently, he and his team had been working for nearly two years, and so far, according to the rumors, the investigation had come up with nothing.

I discovered that the Players Association had refused to supply Mitchell with any of the documents he requested. Executive Director Donald Fehr would agree only to a single interview, while Chief Operating Officer Gene Orza refused to meet with Mitchell at all. The Players Association sent a memo to every active major-league player, informing them they had no legal obligation to cooperate with the investigation and trying everything they could to scare and otherwise discourage players from talking to Mitchell.

Part of the memo the union sent out read: "Any information provided could lead to discipline of you and/or others . . . Remember also there are a number of ongoing federal and state criminal investigations in this area and any information gathered by Senator Mitchell in player interviews is not legally privileged. What that means is that while Senator Mitchell pledges in his memo that he will honor any player requests for confidentiality *in his report*, he does not pledge, because he cannot pledge, that any information you provide will actually remain confidential . . . Senator Mitchell cannot promise that information you disclose will not be given to a federal or state prosecutor, a Congressional committee, or even turned over in a private lawsuit . . .

"A federal prosecutor recently stated in court that the nationwide federal criminal investigations of steroids in sports is ongoing and clearly indicated that the investigation could lead to prosecution of individual athletes for use."

The players didn't dare go against the Players Association. There is no doubt in my mind that the players believed—probably correctly—that if anyone cooperated he would be blackballed from baseball. In fact, the union even offered support to any player named in the Mitchell Report who didn't want to respond to the charges made against him. Basically, the Players Association told its members to keep quiet—but if they were implicated in the report the union would protect them. So after the union made it very clear to players that it didn't want them cooperating with baseball's own investigation, very few players had the guts to risk their career by going against the association.

I really believe that the players who cooperated have been blackballed, including David Segui. He spent fifteen seasons in the major leagues and had a lifetime average of .291. Nobody loves the game more than he does. He built a replica of a major-league stadium on his own land so kids would have a place to play. He would love to get back in the game as a coach, but nobody will talk to him. Maybe it's because of his admitted use of steroids and growth, but more likely it's because he dared tell the truth.

Novitzky told me that, as a result of the memo the union had sent, Senator Mitchell was incredibly frustrated. Both Novitzky and I thought that Mitchell had probably underestimated the difficulty of his job. In a lot of ways, I was his last hope.

We met in the offices of his law firm on Sixth Avenue in Manhattan, right across the street from Radio City Music Hall. Going into the first meeting, I was pretty unhappy about being there. I figured that Mitchell, a former judge and a U.S. senator, was going to think I was just another drug dealer and treat me like one. All of our meetings were held in a crowded conference room. In addition to Senator Mitchell and me, Mitchell's staff was there; and, for legal reasons, prosecutor Matt Parrella, Jeff Novitzky and his partner Irwin Rogers, and FBI special agent Heather Young attended every meeting.

Before my first meeting with Mitchell, Jeff Novitzky told me to prepare a list of all the players I'd dealt with. So I sat down in my basement and began writing down names. And then more names. This was the first time I'd done this, and I was actually surprised how quickly the list grew. Jeff and I compared my list to what the government had compiled from the checks and other papers they had confiscated from my house and the banks. Although legally the government could not provide copies of those checks to Mitchell's private investigation, Jeff helped him as much as he could.

During that first meeting, I sat directly opposite George Mitchell. He was an impressive man, impeccably dressed every time I saw him. In fact throughout the first meeting and the morning session of our second meeting, he wouldn't even loosen his tie.

When I handed Senator Mitchell the list Jeff and I had created he glanced at it quickly, set it down on the table—and then picked it up and literally stared at it. I think he was dumbfounded, because I don't think he had expected it to be so extensive. I could see he was skeptical that I had actually supplied substances to everyone on that list. I'm sure he wondered if I was just trying to gain favor with the government by putting a lot of names down. Senator Mitchell knew that I was facing a substantial prison sentence, so it wasn't beyond reason that I might add some big names to make my role in the scandal seem more important than it actually was. "This is pretty hard to believe," he said, indicating the list. "Can you prove any of it?"

"All of it. I've got canceled checks from every name on that list," I said. I knew what my role in the investigation was going to be— and even with all of Senator Mitchell's accomplishments I wasn't intimidated by him. "Once you see the pattern, you're going to apologize to me."

At that first meeting it was clear Mitchell didn't trust me, and as I had suspected he probably didn't like me very much. All he knew about me was that I had been providing these substances to major leaguers. He acted like a typical lawyer, very cold and abrupt. At times his questions felt much more like an interrogation than an investigation. "I don't have the checks with me," I continued, "but if you need me to, I can get copies and they'll all be for multiples of the same amount, sixteen hundred, thirty-two hundred, and forty-eight hundred dollars. It's all for the same shit."

"You do that and I'll apologize to you," he responded. But even I could tell that he knew that moment changed his entire investigation. Senator Mitchell was only supposed to stay at that first meeting a few hours, because apparently he had meetings scheduled for the afternoon. But once we started talking, he called his secretary and canceled everything. We were in his office till six o'clock; the meeting lasted nine hours. I was told that at the end of that first meeting, after we'd left, his investigators were jumping up and down like they'd won the lottery. After all that time, this was the first major breakthrough they'd gotten.

At the beginning, Senator Mitchell told me how he expected me to handle the questions he was going to ask. "This is a fact-finding mission. We're not here to hurt anybody. All I want from you is the truth, nothing more. I don't want you to leave anything out. Don't minimize or embellish anything. As small as something may seem to you, I want to know it. Don't try to determine what's important; I want to know everything. But don't lie and don't embellish anything."

I told him that I thought we were both there for the same reason. I wanted people to know the truth about what I did and why I did it. I wanted to make it clear to Mitchell, and to everyone else, that I was not some drug dealer, like people believed I was. I promised him, "After we sit down and I go through all of this with you, you're gonna change your mind about me." I told him, "Senator, I'm from the Bronx. I speak my mind. I'm not going to be eloquent. I'm just going to say it the way it is. Don't take it personal if I curse a lot.

I'm not ashamed of that. But what I'm going to do is tell you the truth. I'm not going to lie. I'm going to tell you everything I know, firsthand, just the way it happened."

He remained noncommittal, responding, "If this comes out the way you say it does, then I promise you I'll get your story out." With the prosecutor and chief investigator sitting right next to me, and Senator Mitchell at the long conference table, there was absolutely no way I'd breathe a word that wasn't completely true. I'd been warned that the degree of my cooperation in this investigation would count heavily toward the report they made to my sentencing judge. This, like everything else I was going through, was the line between freedom and jail.

When that first meeting ended, Senator Mitchell asked me to get copies of all my telephone records and my checks as far back as I could. Basically, he wanted the same material that the government already had but that Novitzky and Parrella couldn't legally provide to him. Senator Mitchell offered to pay all the expenses for me, so in a way baseball was paying for the evidence against its own players. I went to every bank that I ever had an account with and sorted through thousands of copied checks. I found a few hundred that had come from players, many of which turned up in the report. But I know for a fact that there were hundreds and hundreds more that I never found.

Senator Mitchell and I met three times in person and had one long phone conversation. Each time I met with his team it was like running a marathon. The investigators focused on the smallest details and challenged everything I said. "How can you prove what this check was for? Why don't you have a receipt for that shipment?

Who did you speak to at that player's phone number?" Trying to remember conversations that had taken place eight or nine years ago, in detail, was very difficult. There were many things I couldn't remember. There were even a couple of players that I had forgotten about totally until the investigators mentioned them by name. There were countless other conversations that I had just forgotten about.

In addition to discussing the players on my list, Senator Mitchell asked me if I had any information about a lot of other players, often making it obvious that he had heard rumors about them or had been told by baseball that some of these players had tested positive for steroids. He had suspicions, but he needed hard evidence. He particularly asked me about all the big stars who had been the subject of whispered rumors. Their names were not secret: Pudge Rodríguez, Randy Johnson, Curt Schilling, Alex Rodriguez, Gary Sheffield. I told him that, like everybody else, I'd heard their names linked anecdotally to steroids, but I personally had never dealt with any of them and had no firsthand evidence that they was using.

When the investigators asked me my personal opinion about whether those guys were using juice, I made it very clear that this was only my personal opinion and applied to the majority of major leaguers, not just A-Rod or Sheffield or anybody else specifically: "All you've got to do is look at his body. A-Rod played with a lot of people that I know were using. What would make him so special that he wouldn't try it? And if he wanted to stay on top, why wouldn't he? Listen, if you're playing with or against guys who are all doing it and they're hitting the shit out of the ball and you're in a slump, what are you gonna do? I'm A-Rod and I'm in a slump and some guy who can't carry my jock is hitting twenty-five home runs? I'm not going to try it? Come on, what do you think?"

What I wanted Senator Mitchell and his team to understand was how prevalent these substances were in baseball and the reasons that players decided to use them. But the more we talked about what was going on in baseball, the more it became clear to me how little they really understood about the culture of the major leagues.

During those meetings it also became obvious to me why Senator Mitchell had been so successful. He had a way of making a person feel comfortable, even when the discussion got tense. He was always calm, always low key; in a room full of people he would look at me and make me feel like we were having a private conversation just between the two of us. Although he had been defensive during our first meeting, after lunch on the second day we met, while he still wore his sports jacket, I could see he had loosened his tie. I took that as a sign that his attitude toward me had changed; I think finally he had accepted the fact that I was telling him the truth. I can't begin to guess how many questions either he or his assistants asked me, but as he had warned me, they wanted every single detail. We talked for hours, discussing player after player after player as well as things that seemed obvious and unimportant to me. For a while we talked about logistics. For example, for each player I named Mitchell and his guys wanted to know how I delivered the individual packages. I didn't think much of it at the time, but I later learned that the delivery method was important because it affected the distribution charge I had against me.

While the general atmosphere was that we were doing something important, there was no excitement, no glamour, no sense that we were doing anything extraordinary. Sometimes it seemed like grunt work, just going over and over the tiniest details of what I'd done. While I wasn't happy about any of it, answering Mitchell's questions didn't make me depressed like Novitzky's investigation had. Mostly, it was drudgery. In all our sessions the only time we laughed was when Mitchell and his investigators found the check sent to me by Rondell White—the one on which he'd written on the bottom, "bought something."

After Senator Mitchell had asked me every conceivable question about the checks, we went through thousands of telephone numbers to find out who I was talking to and when. The investigators uncovered incredibly small details, like the one time I called Kevin Brown at his mother's house.

Once in a while Mitchell would ask me a question that Matt Parrella interrupted. He would say, "Let's go outside for a second," which meant the government had some information Parrella wanted to share that I wasn't supposed to know. When that happened everyone left the room except Senator Mitchell and me. The two of us would talk man-to-man for a few minutes. That was the only time I talked about my real feelings.

During the second meeting, it had become painfully obvious to me that Mitchell's investigation had gone nowhere until I had agreed to cooperate. When everyone else was outside, I told the senator in a low voice, "I don't want to be the only one thrown under a bus. I see what's going on and so far I'm the only one getting fucked here."

Senator Mitchell understood. He repeated his promise to me: "If everything you tell us turns out to be true, when it comes time your name will be cleared."

My guess is that the thing that most surprised Senator Mitchell and his investigators was that I continued to defend of the use of steroids and growth by baseball players. I never backed down about that. Usually when a person has pleaded guilty to a crime and is facing a prison sentence, they either claim they didn't do it or admit that they had made a terrible mistake. I didn't do any of that. I admitted my guilt and agreed that I would never, ever, sell or give away or distribute controlled substances of any type. But unlike everyone else who has been involved in this whole scandal, I also told them that I didn't understand why these drugs are illegal and I didn't understand what was so wrong about players wanting to recover faster than usual so they could get back to the job they're being paid to do.

By our third meeting, Senator Mitchell seemed even more relaxed, though he was never quite casual. During a break in that meeting, he confided to me that his investigators had checked out a lot of the things I'd told them, and from what he could tell it was confirmed by other sources. "Boy," he said, I think with amazement, "no one is disputing you."

During these meetings, just like when I had been talking to Novitzky, I was often able to figure out from the questions investigators asked who else was cooperating and at least some of what they had learned. For example, when Senator Mitchell asked me, "Who's the person at Lexus that you know?" I instantly knew that my friend Brian McNamee was cooperating.

On December 11, 2007, two days before the Mitchell Report

was scheduled to be released, all the people who had been to our previous meetings got together on a final conference call that lasted about two hours. During this call Senator Mitchell went over several points he was going to make, and then asked me specific questions again about some of baseball's biggest stars. In most cases he had good information that these players had used performance-enhancing drugs, but he hadn't been able to confirm it from a second source. He wanted me to search my memory to make sure there was nothing I could add to these stories. The rule I'd made for myself right at the beginning was that if I didn't deal directly with a player I wasn't going to give up his name. I wasn't going to repeat stories that I didn't know were true. All I told Senator Mitchell was that "I've heard the same stories about these guys and I've got my own opinion. But I can't confirm them." Since Senator Mitchell couldn't confirm what he had heard, those players weren't named in the final report.

As we neared the end of the call, Senator Mitchell thanked me for my help and warned me about the media storm that would follow when the report was released. Until this call I didn't have any idea how much of what I'd told him was going to appear in the report. Basically, without me they had almost nothing. Without my participation, the almost four-hundred-page report probably would have been about fifty pages long. A media storm, I thought to myself? Prepared? I laughed to myself. I'd been standing naked in the center of a media hurricane for almost a year.

So I thought I knew what to expect on the day the Mitchell Report was released. Even though I had played a part in the preparation of it, I never saw the final report. When I read the first sentence,

I knew Senator Mitchell and his team had gotten it right: "For more than a decade there has been widespread illegal use of anabolic steroids and other performance enhancing substances by players in Major League Baseball . . ." At the bottom of the first page Senator Mitchell concluded, "Each of the thirty clubs has had players who have been involved with performance enhancing substances at some time in their careers."

I stopped after reading the first page. Believe it or not, I wasn't that interested in reading the whole thing. When I saw how many pages long it was, there was no way I was going to print it out. I knew it would take two cartridges and two reams of paper. And since I'd told Mitchell a lot of what he'd written, I figured I already knew much of what was in the report. My friends who did read it, though, told me that I was mentioned throughout the whole thing and that Senator Mitchell was extremely complimentary about my contribution, which made me happy. I had also fulfilled another obligation under the plea agreement, which took me another big step farther away from a jail sentence.

In fact, I've never sat down and read it from cover to cover, even to this day. But in preparation for writing my story, I really needed to know specifically what Senator Mitchell had included and what he'd left out. So I read through sections of it, especially those parts that discussed the individual players I'd dealt with.

Meanwhile the media assault began even before reporters had a chance to read the whole report. I'd tried to warn my friend Brian McNamee about what was going to happen, but as he later told me, "Just hearing about it couldn't possibly prepare me for what happened." The reporting herd descended on his house like locusts, only worse. They tracked his movements by helicopter, literally climbed over the fences into his backyard, and looked in his windows. Like mine, his phone never stopped ringing.

I was never concerned about the public's reaction to the report. I had discovered from my own experience that good people are always good people and assholes don't change. Unfortunately, when the report was first released Senator Mitchell's staff had forgotten to black out my home phone number on a few receipts that they included at the end, so I began receiving calls from people screaming, "I want to buy steroids!" and then hanging up, as well as from people asking me if I would autograph their copy of the Mitchell Report, and also a few threats.

But the people who mattered in my life were all tremendously supportive. None of them wavered at all. Even strangers generally were very nice. I was surprised that so many people recognized me on the street, and when someone did, most nodded or smiled or gave me a thumbs-up; there wasn't a single unpleasant incident. I'd also recently started working out at a new gym, and the culture at the gym remained that you don't bother someone when he's working out, even if he's on the cover of the newspaper. So nobody bothered me there either.

I went about my life and my business after the report was published, doing my best to avoid reporters. Three weeks after it was issued, I had to go to Senator Mitchell's office to meet with representatives of the United States Olympic Committee, who wanted to ask me questions about left-handed pitcher Jeff Williams, who had played for Australia in the 1996 and 2004 games. When Senator Mitchell saw me, he invited me into his private office for the first time. It was just the two of us. He didn't say it, but I think he was happy with the overall response to his report, both from the general public and the media. He'd busted open baseball's secret society, and for the first time the full extent of steroid and growth hormone use had been revealed—even though I knew it was more prevalent than Senator Mitchell had been able to prove. This time players who were named lost. When we were alone in his office I said to Senator Mitchell, "I'd like to thank you for what you wrote about me."

He said, "Kirk, as I told you from the very beginning, I just wanted the truth." He didn't say so, but I think Senator Mitchell was very pleased he'd been able to complete his work after baseball and the Players Association had tried their hardest to make it difficult for him. He had played their game and beat them at it. He'd won; baseball and the union had lost.

The media focused almost completely on the players named in the report and nearly ignored the conclusions Senator Mitchell reached. When I heard about the players he'd named, I was both surprised and even a little confused. There were several players I told him I'd dealt with who weren't named in the report, and I couldn't figure out why. Maybe it was because I didn't remember who had introduced me to the player, or I hadn't supplied written proof and Senator Mitchell hadn't been able to verify it. Or it's possible that those players had ignored the association and spoken to him. A few were career minor leaguers most people have never heard of; others were journeyman players who had used growth for recovery. A couple of my guys probably tried it once and explained that to Mitchell. I don't have an explanation; I gave him the names,

I gave him whatever evidence I hadn't thrown out, and he made the decision. The truth is that the names he left out aren't big names. They aren't the superstars that the media was looking for. He's a senator, the man who turned down a nomination to the Supreme Court. I've got a nice car-detailing business out on Long Island. I'm not about to question his decisions.

Naturally, baseball as an industry embraced Senator Mitchell's conclusions and promised to make the necessary changes to the testing program and to enforce the rules against substance abuse. Although there's very little about any of this that's funny, I have to admit that I found the response from Donald Fehr, the executive director of the Players Association, pretty humorous. In a statement released a few weeks after the report, Fehr complained, "Many players are named, their reputations adversely affected forever. Anyone interested in fairly assessing the allegations against a player should consider the nature of the evidence presented, the reliability of its source, and the absence of procedural safeguards individuals who may be accused of wrongdoing should be afforded."

"The nature of the evidence" was basically the checks and taped conversations that I provided as well as the verbal admissions of several players. As for the "the reliability of its source," I assume that was me. While I was prepared to get sued for what was attributed to me in the Mitchell Report, there were no lawsuits filed against me. There is very little that is funny about these events, too many lives were affected—particularly mine—but reading about Fehr complaining that the players didn't have adequate "procedural safeguards" was funny. It's my opinion that the Players Association was totally responsible for the fact that "many players are named."

The union probably could have provided better safeguards if it had worked with Senator Mitchell instead of blocking him.

Fehr added that if any player was disciplined the Players Association would make sure he received "a hearing and the full panoply of due process protections our agreements contemplate, and we will represent him in that process." To me that certainly seemed like warming up a relief pitcher after the game was over.

After the Mitchell Report was released, Jeff Novitzky's office received several calls from official athletic organizations requesting my cooperation on substance abuse–related investigations. In addition to the request to testify in front of Congress, which I rejected, the Olympic Committee that wanted to talk to me about Jeff Williams, the Australian athlete suspected of using steroids when the Aussies won a silver medal in 2004—if they could prove he was using a banned substance, the medal could be taken away from him—asked if I would be willing to fly to Australia to testify.

I remembered Jeff Williams. In my deposition to the government I'd admitted that I spoke with him twice, three times tops. I believe Adam Riggs gave Williams my phone number when he was getting ready to go to Japan to play for the Hanshin Tigers. I had no idea who he was when he first called. I asked him, "Are you a pitcher?"

"Yeah, I'm in Japan now," he said, and we talked for a while. Williams picked my brain, but I could tell he knew about steroids, so I guessed that he had used them before. He told me he wanted to put a little more weight on, but he didn't want to take shots.

I explained to him, "You know you limit yourself when you don't take shots. There are a couple of pills you could do that'll put weight on and a couple will give you more strength, with the combination you can do both. Start with one and end with the other and you should get good results."

He understood. I sent him Dianabol, which builds mass and allows you to put on weight, and Anavar, a cutting drug that does not put on weight. I may have also sent him a kit, but I'm not certain about that. I had a check from him. I read that he passed all the drug tests in the Olympics and the committee did not follow up on my deposition. The president of the Hanshin Tigers defended him, telling the media, "He flatly denied the use of any banned substances and said he is ready to accept fresh checkups at any time."

The day before I was to be sentenced, I met with representatives of the Olympic Committee for the second time, this time in San Francisco. I told them the truth, that I hadn't supplied Williams with any substance within a time frame that could have been effective during the Olympics. The Olympic Committee declined to take any action against Williams, and that was the last time I participated in any investigation concerning performance-enhancing drugs and sports.

All my life I'd heard the saying, "Today is the first day of the rest of your life," but never did it mean more to me than after the Mitchell Report was released. I was a free man, living happily with my family in my home on Long Island. I was more than ready to let go of the past, and fortunately most of the media agreed with me and left me alone. Unfortunately for my friend Brian McNamee, his trial in front of the American public was just beginning.

NINE

I never once considered the possibility that I would be invited to testify in front of the United States Congress. But after the Mitchell Report was issued, the House Committee on Oversight and Government Reform wrote and called my lawyer, John Reilly, several times in order to invite me to appear and answer its questions. That was an invitation I could refuse, and I did.

This was the same committee that had held hearings into the use of steroids in baseball in 2005, and when the Mitchell Report proved those hearings were a joke, the congressmen knew they had to do something to save their reputations. For example, during that 2005 hearing Rafael Palmeiro testified under oath that he had never used performance-enhancing drugs—and a few months later he was suspended by baseball for ten days after testing positive for exactly the same drugs he'd just denied using. He wasn't the only player to sit there and look those people in the face and deny using drugs despite a lot of circumstantial evidence: Miguel Tejada acknowledged self-injecting vitamin B-12 dozens of times but told the committee that he had never used steroids and didn't know anyone who did, even though he was friendly with Adam

Piatt, who admitted to the committee that he bought kits from me both for his personal use and for his teammate Tejada. It seemed to me that the purpose of these hearings was the same as it had been three years before: they allowed members of Congress to get their pictures in newspapers and appear on TV. I knew nothing would be different this time.

While there was a part of me that wanted to make use of the national stage to defend myself, the fact was that legally I could put myself in jeopardy. Since testifying in front of Congress had not been part of my plea agreement with the government, it was up to me to decide what I wanted to do.

My attorney told Congress, Kirk won't answer a single question unless you give him complete immunity. If the government had granted me full immunity, I would have answered any question it asked, completely and honestly. If it refused to grant me immunity, but still subpoenaed me, I was going to invoke my Fifth Amendment rights to keep my mouth shut.

Congress refused to grant me immunity. To me it felt like being invited to my own hanging and then asked, "Oh, by the way, please bring your own rope." The government told Reilly that it couldn't grant me immunity because then it would have to give it to everyone who testified.

Without immunity, I wasn't going to answer a single question, which made it silly for the committee to subpoena me. But my friend Brian McNamee made a different decision. He decided to testify. He told me that since he had already testified so many times, he decided to accept the "challenge," as he referred to it, because, "After everything that has been said about me, I knew it couldn't get any worse." After what happened to Brian at those hearings, it was obvious that I'd made the right decision.

Brian McNamee is a New York trainer who, as I've mentioned, had become a close friend. Eventually, the two of us found ourselves together at the center of the scandal. I had often supplied Brian with steroids and growth for his own clients, so after I was arrested, in an effort to protect a friend, I had stopped talking to him. Our relationship went back to 1999, when Brian was the Toronto Blue Jays' strength coach and was training David Segui, who introduced us. David had told Brian that I was a very good trainer and had a lot of knowledge about steroids, and we spoke on the phone many times.

Brian and I actually met in person about a year later, when he was working for the Yankees and decided to buy himself a Lexus. I told him I had a good contact at a local Lexus dealership, so when Senator Mitchell asked that question about who I knew at Lexus, it was obvious to me that Brian had started talking to him.

When we met in the Lexus showroom, neither one of us could have imagined in our wildest dreams that only a few years later Brian would be named the trainer for *Sports Illustrated*'s All-Scandal Team—right in front of the Pittsburgh Pirates Parrot—and then end up testifying in front of a congressional committee.

David told me that Brian was a total stand-up guy, and he definitely is. I know the image that the media created of Brian, but the truth is that he's a smart, hardworking, honest person and an excellent trainer. The major damage to Brian's reputation dated back to 2001, when he was accused of giving a girl the date rape drug, GHB, and having sex with her in a pool while she was passed out.

But I knew the truth was that Brian had taken the fall on that charge to protect someone associated with the Yankees organization. He'd lied to protect someone else: a perfect example of what happens to a lot of people who work for baseball clubs. The first rule is to protect the team by protecting the player. Later it came out that the girl was covering an affair she was having with a married Yankee player. There was a witness who claimed that the girl would have drowned if Brian hadn't helped her get out of the pool. But that accusation had gotten a ton of publicity and there were a lot of people who believed it. The people who really knew Brian knew it couldn't be true; that isn't the type of person he is.

In those days we would talk to each other often, but almost never about steroids or growth. Just about everything the general public knows about me and Brian is based on the fact that we were involved with steroids. In the minds of the public that's who we are, baseball's drug pushers; but really we were just two normal men who were passionate about fitness and worked in that industry. We'd sit for hours, talking about training techniques and weight programs and all the other things generally associated with physical training. We'd talk about our families and how much it was costing to get our cars fixed and everything else that two friends who speak on a regular basis discuss.

When I met Brian he knew very little about steroids beyond the fact that they existed, that they were popular around the gym, and that some players were using them. In fact he told me that in 1998 he'd begun injecting Roger Clemens with Winstrol that Clemens had gotten for himself. Since Brian didn't know very much about steroids, when Clemens got a bottle of Anadrol and asked him about it, Brian decided to approach someone he thought would know about it, José Canseco, for information. Canseco voluntarily took the bottle from Brian.

The first ballplayer Brian connected me to was Jason Grimsley, and Brian probably didn't even know it when it happened. One day in the locker room before a game, Grimsley showed Brian some really bad Winstrol and asked his opinion. When Brian warned him, "You really shouldn't be taking that crap," Jason asked him if he knew where he could get better steroids. Brian put him in touch with Segui, who gave him my number.

After Brian and I became friends, though, every time one of his clients in baseball would ask him a question about steroids he would come to me for the answer. "How would you respond to this?" he'd ask, or "What's the best thing for a reliever to use?" but he would never mention the player's name. Instead he'd say, "One of my people wants to do this. What should I tell him?" As I told the government, everything Brian learned about steroids, he learned from me.

I know that Brian never pushed steroids, but like every other personal trainer, he had to learn about them because his clients were asking questions. If Brian couldn't answer those questions, he would have been out of the game. His clients would hire someone more knowledgeable—and maybe someone who could get stuff for them. As a former cop, Brian was pretty knowledgeable about the law, so both of us knew that what we were doing was illegal and what the consequences of our transactions could be. Because of those risks we were both careful never to mention the players we supplied substances to by name. That gave us plausible deniability. But I knew his list of clients, so it wasn't hard to guess that Roger Clemens, Andy Pettitte, and infielder Chuck Knoblauch were probably juicing.

Brian started buying steroids and growth hormones from me in 2000 and continued for more than four years, but only when one of his clients asked him to get them. While Brian never told me specifically who he was buying what for, he would drop pretty big hints. For example, if Clemens or Knoblauch got hot for a little while, he would say something to me like, "He's on the program now." Any doubt I might have had about who was using the products I supplied to Brian ended when he asked me to send a couple of kits to him at Clemens's home address.

Even though Brian got very close to Clemens and his family, and Clemens was paying a sizeable amount of his salary, I know that Brian never completely trusted him. He liked him a lot, and I know that he lied for him, but I think Brian always knew that Roger's first loyalty was to Roger. In fact when it became clear that the government was going to start an investigation, I remember Brian telling me, "You watch, if anything ever happens Pettitte's going to be the guy who sticks up for me; Roger's gonna take a walk. Andy's going to come out and say 'I did it,' and Roger's going to deny, deny, deny. Roger always made it clear that I was his employee, not his friend." In fact Brian was so certain that Roger would do whatever was necessary to protect himself that he saved empty bottles and syringes that Clemens had used in his basement.

Unfortunately, the government caught Brian through me. Novitzky found copies of his checks in my records. I'd sold him growth and steroids. Brian was the only person I warned that the investigators had his name, even though I didn't plan on telling him. He'd called me several times after Novitzky had raided my house, and to try to protect him I hadn't returned his calls, so he knew something was going on. One day I happened to run into him out in Queens and he confronted me. "What's wrong?" he asked. "How come I haven't heard from you?"

It was a really difficult situation for me and I tried to blow him off. I said, "You know, I got a lot of shit going on." I was unusually cold and curt with him. I really didn't want to talk. I knew Novitzky would be talking to him soon. Then Brian called me at work out of the blue and caught me off guard. "Look," I warned him, "they got me." I didn't have to tell Brian who "they" were, because after Jason Grimsley's story had become public, Brian knew all about Jeff Novitzky and the ongoing investigation. I continued, "They're probably going to come visit you and ask questions. Don't lie to them. I don't want to get you in a jam, but I had to tell them the whole truth. I told them that you bought kits from me but that I didn't know where they went. Just tell them the whole truth." Maybe I shouldn't have said anything, but I knew that eventually the government had to go after Brian. I also gave Novitzky's phone number to Brian in case he wanted to speak with him directly.

That was the last time Brian and I spoke until after I was sentenced. The government had warned me not to talk to him because it didn't want us to collaborate on our stories. But I felt a little better when I figured out from Senator Mitchell's questions that he had spoken to Brian and that Brian was telling him the whole truth. I found out later that Brian had signed his own agreement with the government that stipulated he would not be charged with distributing steroids as long as he told prosecutors the complete and absolute truth. The stories I was telling Senator Mitchell only confirmed Brian's testimony. In fact our stories matched so completely that Senator Mitchell couldn't believe that we never talked. But we didn't; we just both told the truth.

Throughout all our legal maneuverings, Brian and I communicated only through Novitzky, who was talking to both of us. Sometimes he would tell me things like, "Brian wanted me to say hello and tell you he's praying for you." I'd ask Jeff to relay similar messages to him.

Brian was the second person I called after I had been sentenced, after I had spoken to my family first. Although Brian and I hadn't spoken in more than a year, circumstances had made us closer than we'd ever been. Our first conversation lasted more than two hours. During that conversation Brian told me that he had agreed to testify in the forthcoming congressional hearings. "What about you?" he asked. "You going to go to Washington?"

That's when I told him that I wouldn't testify without being given immunity.

While everybody expected me to testify after the Mitchell Report came out, I watched the hearings on TV, and it seemed even more ridiculous than I suspected it would be. The day before Roger Clemens and Brian testified, Clemens went on some sort of bizarre victory tour and visited nineteen members of the committee so the congressmen could get his autograph or have photos taken with him. Apparently, Roger is a friend of President George W. Bush from the time Bush was part owner of the Texas Rangers, and Roger was a contributor to his political campaigns. But it was absolutely disgraceful to me the way those committee members fawned over him, because these were the same people who were going to question him the next day and eventually have to make some sort of judgment about whether or not he was telling the truth.

When I talked to Brian, it turned out that he wasn't bothered by it as much as I was; he actually thought the whole spectacle was funny. "When it comes down to it," Brian told me, "I'll out-testify his ass any day in cross-examination." According to Brian, Clemens was basing his appearance on "ego, arrogance, and entitlement," while Brian was just going to tell the truth.

The next day Roger Clemens actually surprised Brian. While Brian knew that if it became necessary Roger wasn't going to defend him, he really didn't expect him to sit there and lie.

Brian told the committee the same thing he'd sworn to in his deposition, that he'd injected Clemens with steroids numerous times, including—as he swore in that deposition—once in a pantry storage room in the Tampa Bay ballpark, "where they kept all the extra chips and cookies and stuff for the clubhouse . . . but I injected him too quickly, because it was like hurry, go, get out. I mean, who wants to see two guys getting out of the storage room?"

When Clemens finally got the opportunity to testify, he said flatly, "I have never taken steroids and HGH." After that strong denial—and then claiming that his wife, Debbie, had actually been injected with the growth hormones Brian had purchased from me—Clemens pointed toward Brian and said, "I have strong disagreements with what this man says about me."

While Clemens was testifying, people watching could see Brian scribbling on a congressional pad. To most of those people it probably looked like he was making notes about Clemens's statements, but that really wasn't what he was doing. Brian told me that he and his lawyers were playing games of hangman. I asked him if he remembered the secret words he picked. "Yeah," he said, "'criminal' and 'liar.'"

Like Brian had told me he would, he out-testified Roger's ass. "I injected those drugs into the body of Roger Clemens at his direction," he said. Then he pointed out, "I have no reason to lie and every reason not to. If I do lie, I'll be prosecuted. I told the investigators that I injected three people, two of whom, I believe, confirm my account. The third is sitting at this table."

When Andy Pettitte's testimony backed up everything Brian said, Clemens suggested that Pettitte probably "misremembers" what happened.

At the conclusion of the hearings, though, nothing happened. The Republicans sided with Clemens, the Democrats sided with Brian, and the members of the committee got their publicity. The whole thing was a joke. If they actually wanted to accomplish something, they would have subpoenaed several team owners and questioned them under oath. The owner of the Giants, Peter McGowan, at one point admitted he knew what was going on in regard to steroids and then later changed his statement. I believe Congress didn't want to hear the truth because then it would have been forced to take some actions.

One thing is clear: either Brian or Roger lied under oath to the Congress of the United States. That's perjury, and normal people, who don't pitch in the major leagues, are sent to prison for it every day. If the committee was so interested in getting to the truth, it should have investigated who was lying. But Congress did nothing, and why it hasn't taken action is as obvious to me as those autographed pictures of Clemens hanging on their office walls.

But Congress isn't the only institution that should be blamed. In my opinion, major-league baseball is most at fault. I know from my own experience that baseball intentionally looked the other way for years in regard to the use of steroids, human growth hormones, and other substances.

Roger Clemens wasn't the only player to lie about using this stuff; it's just that he did it on national television. Throughout this entire investigation, and especially after the release of the Mitchell Report, players had been going out of their way to deny that they knew me or that they had used any of these substances. And each and every one of those players was lying.

TEN

In October 2008 the federal court in San Francisco decided that the Players Association had the legal right to keep private the names of the ninety players who came up positive in the survey testing in 2003. That was five years after the testing was done, but it's still being argued in court. I'm certain that a lot of those players aren't even in the big leagues anymore, so it really doesn't matter if their names get released. Even for active players, there won't be any penalties. In fact one of the things that really surprised me is how many players who got caught or were named in the Mitchell Report have either denied using steroids or growth hormones or made up ridiculous stories to try to explain what they were doing.

After the existence of my recordings was made public, only one player claimed that somehow the calls weren't accurate, and that was left-handed relief pitcher Ron Villone. He was a journeyman pitcher, a middle reliever who stayed in the big leagues because he could get out lefties. In eleven big-league seasons Villone had never played for the same team more than two years in a row, and after the 2005 season, the Marlins traded him to the Yankees. Denny Neagle had introduced us when Villone was with Seattle and he'd bought growth from me several times. I think Villone was having some problems with his back when he called me. I remember that once I sent two kits directly to the Mariners clubhouse for him. He was a Jersey guy, so once I met him in a diner not far from my house and handed him a package. I remember that Villone, for some reason, would send me cash tucked inside the pages of a Seattle Mariners yearbook. Our conversations were pretty straightforward, since he knew what he wanted and I could get it for him. But after his name was released, he said that he "did see some inaccuracies, but that's a he-said, she-said and I'm not going to get into that." Villone also told reporters that he did not intend to take any legal action about those "inaccuracies." I don't know what kind of inaccuracies there could be, since Villone's voice is recorded on the tape, begging me to send him growth hormones.

Maybe the strangest explanation of all came from pitcher Jim Parque, who told the *Chicago Sun-Times*, "Either someone isn't telling the truth or steroids really don't work because I was throwing 80, 81 mph before the report said I took them, and I was throwing 80, 81 mph after I allegedly took them. You have a guy trying to plea bargain to save his own ass, so of course he's going to throw as many names as possible out there." But Parque's denial really wasn't believable, because I was able to produce two checks from him for forty-eight hundred dollars. Even though he told the reporter, "I don't even know this Kirk guy," Parque admitted writing the checks, but claimed they were for, "a bunch of supplements, some creatine, vitamins, some stuff to increase my red-blood-cell count and some herbs from South America that were supposed to help with my injuries." South American herbs? My freedom is at stake based on the degree of my cooperation with Senator Mitchell, and I would decide that I could clinch the deal by lying to him about Jim Parque, because I knew that just mentioning his name would impress everybody?

Probably the denial that surprised me the most, though, was from David Justice. I only met him once, after the 2000 World Series, but I remember it very well. The Yankees were holding an autograph show in Jersey, so as a favor to a friend I picked up Justice there and drove him to the airport. Even during that short drive, it was obvious that he knew what he was doing in regard to steroids. I'd heard from other players that Justice was juicing, although I had no idea where he was getting it. But Justice knew what substances he wanted, how to use them all, and didn't ask me any questions about taking shots. All I did was recommend what dosage would be best for him. He'd told me what he wanted and I'd brought it for him, plus some extra in case he changed his mind. Justice ended up buying almost everything I had with me. I probably sold him four or five boxes of growth and as many as fifty Decas, a big box of stuff.

Justice was one of the few players who agreed to speak with Senator Mitchell, but the mistake he made was meeting with Mitchell before I had been interviewed. Apparently, Justice told investigators about other players he suspected were using but admitted he had no direct knowledge of those players' steroid use—and then he claimed that he didn't use performance-enhancing substances himself. When his name was included in the report, Justice was all over the media, strongly stating that the Mitchell Report was inaccurate. He even urged other players whose names were made public to strongly deny my allegations; Justice even made a point of urging Roger Clemens to stand up against the allegations. Well, we know how good that advice turned out to be for Roger.

I never saw David Justice actually take any of the substances he purchased from me, but one of my other clients, Glenallen Hill, told me that Justice had admitted to him that he was using juice. Besides, it's almost impossible to believe he'd buy so much stuff from me and then decide not to use it. I didn't have copies of a check from him, so I suspect Justice thought he could bluff his way out of it. After all, without physical evidence it was his word against mine. It was the same old arrogance: he was a major-league star, and I was a clubhouse guy; which one of us are the fans going to believe? But when Senator Mitchell bolstered my credibility by stating that everything I'd told him that could be investigated had proved to be true, Justice closed his mouth. The big difference between Justice and me was that I was under oath. If I lied I was going to prison; if he lied, nothing would happen to him. I think that stacks a deck pretty strongly.

What I couldn't understand was why players like Justice would even bother to deny the accusations. It was pretty obvious to everyone that baseball wanted to do whatever it could to make this whole mess disappear as rapidly as possible and that the Players Association was going to fight whatever minor penalties anyone might try to impose. Maybe the players figured that if they admitted to using steroids their reputations would be destroyed. But that wasn't, and isn't, the case, because baseball fans forgive their idols, period. Just look at Jason Giambi.

I can honestly understand, however, why a player like outfielder

Gary Sheffield, who has had a career that should put him in the Hall of Fame, might protest his guilt. Admitting he used performance-enhancing substances would certainly delay his inauguration and might even prevent it. The sportswriters who vote for the Hall of Fame punish players for their actions. In Sheffield's case, it actually was better to deny, deny, deny. I had no direct dealings with him, but I believed he was using because of the people he hung around with. In his own book he wrote, "I had no interest in steroids, I didn't need them and I didn't want them . . ." He claimed that he had "never touched a strength-building steroid in my life—and never will." His problem was that the investigators had records of him dealing with BALCO. He explained that the bill he had received from BALCO was actually for vitamins, and that he didn't know whether or not the "cream"—which was BALCO's steroid that you rubbed on like lotion—Bonds had admitted to using actually contained steroids. In other words, BALCO made him do it. At least he didn't claim he was using South American herbs.

Matt Franco is another player who was clearly not destined for the Hall of Fame, so I don't know why he denied buying or using steroids. I met Franco when he was with the Mets, where he had a nice career as a pinch hitter. It was a little surprising when Franco told Senator Mitchell that he had never met me, talked to me, bought anything from me, or knew who I was before he read about my guilty plea. Apparently, I'm not that memorable. I remember it differently. I remember when I unexpectedly ran into Franco at an autographing event in a shopping center. There were a few hundred people waiting in line. I was walking by his table and he looked up and saw me and said, "Kirk, what's going on?" I stopped and we talked for a few minutes; he asked for my phone number and called me a few days later. He wanted some Deca, but he bought so little that it was more of a joke than a purchase. It was like a sip from a full twelve-ounce glass of water. I assumed he was just trying everything to extend his career one season longer. But for him to deny even knowing me is silly. Maybe it's just his ego, maybe he feels it's important for people to know that he was a solid major-league player without taking any enhancements, but either he has an extremely poor memory or he isn't telling the truth.

Another player who shouldn't have any reason to deny his involvement with me is Hal Morris. When Senator Mitchell was in the middle of his investigation, Hal Morris's lawyer wrote to him, and the correspondence said that his client "denied the use of anabolic steroids, testosterone and/or human growth hormones during his major league career." Now, that might technically be accurate, since my memory is that Morris bought steroids from me at the conclusion of his career, and I have no idea when he actually used them. Morris was very typical of the players I dealt with; I didn't know him very well and he only bought a little from me. I think I may have spoken to him twice. I met him in '97 or '98 after I'd left the Mets, although at that point I wasn't doing any business with him. He called me at the end of 1999, when he was getting out of baseball, which was what made the call so unusual. At the time, Morris told me that he was thinking about retiring and wanted to do one more push. This was just before growth hormones were available, so I sent him steroids, Deca and tes. I don't remember ever talking to Morris again after I got that stuff for him.

Darren Holmes had an unusual excuse. While he admitted that

he had ordered growth hormones from one of those online rejuvenation centers, he claimed that the steroids he received were sent to him by mistake, that he never ordered them, but that the kit was mistakenly included in the delivery. Supposedly, when Holmes found them in the package he decided not to use them and just threw them away. In fairness, I didn't see him use anything, and it's certainly possible he's telling the truth. Personally, though, his story is very hard for me to believe.

Glenallen Hill was another player who admitted he had bought steroids from me but claimed he'd never used them. Hill was a former player who had to speak with Mitchell's investigators because he works in baseball as a coach. He told investigators that he got my phone number from a player named David in 2000. The Mitchell Report quotes it as follows: "Hill said that 'David' admitted using steroids and was knowledgeable about its effects and the different types of anabolic steroids." According to the report, he also said that "'David' was the only individual who ever admitted to him that he used performance enhancing substances." Most people assumed that "David" was David Segui. But I think "David" is David Justice. I met Glenallen Hill at the same card show in Jersey at which I met Justice. After that, Hill called me about five times. I remember he was pretty knowledgeable about both growth and steroids. During one of our conversations, Hill mentioned that he'd bought some growth hormones from someone in San Francisco but he didn't seem to get any benefit from them. "It was nothing," he said. "It didn't work."

"Let me ask you," I said, "did your feet swell up? Did you get any tingling in your hands?"

"No, nothing," Hill replied. I asked him exactly what he'd been using. He told me the brand name so I knew it was a quality product. "It probably died on you," I told him, which meant that the drug hadn't been stored properly. Growth hormones are really sensitive, and if they are left in sunlight or heat they will "die." It's worthless, because when the hormones are finally mixed with water, the drug won't "wake up." But if it's stored properly, in a dark place and at a constant temperature, growth will last as long as a week after it's mixed. In other words, growth can't be kept in the glove compartment of a car. I used to advise my clients that if it was already mixed when their team went on the road, they should go to any pharmacy and buy a diabetic pack, which is intended to keep insulin and other drugs cold. I offered to send Hill a new bottle of good stuff to try, and after he had used it, Hill called again to tell me it had worked.

But apparently Hill forgot all about it, because while he admitted to Mitchell's investigators that he'd bought a steroid, Sustanon, from me, he also claimed that he didn't use it because he was going through some personal problems. Instead of using what I sent him, Hill said he put it away and never remembered that he had it—for six years! Hill told Mitchell's people that he had discovered the unopened bottle in 2007 when he was unpacking after moving. Maybe he's telling the truth, too—perhaps they all are, since none of the players admitted to using what they received from me. But it's the biggest streak of bad luck I've ever heard.

Infielder Fernando Viña was another one of my customers with a poor memory. I met Viña when he was in the Mets' minor-league system. We were about the same age, and in spring training he was one of the players who always asked the clubbies questions. Most frequently, "Did I make the team?" We became friends and since Viña was with the Mets before anybody used steroids much, I didn't sell him anything until he was with the Brewers in the late 1990s. Viña asked for my number when I saw him at a game, and I knew what he wanted. When he called, he had the usual goals: put on some weight, get his strength up, and heal some injuries. I helped him for a long period of time. Once a year I'd hear from him; he never bought a lot, just enough to maintain. I made six or seven sales of steroids to him and then sold him three or four kits over a short period of time because he'd hurt his hamstring.

By the time Fernando Viña's name appeared in the Mitchell Report, he had retired after twelve big-league seasons and become a popular broadcaster on ESPN's *Baseball Tonight*, so maybe he did have something to lose by telling the truth. After he was named, Viña went on ESPN and claimed that he hadn't bought steroids from me. He did admit, however, that he had bought growth hormones to help recover from an injury. I guess Viña thought that HGH wasn't as serious as steroids. It didn't matter; he was still lying about the steroids. It was both funny and sad watching him on TV, trying to look comfortable while he denied the truth. Viña could deny it all he wanted to, but he had to make up excuses to explain the checks I had from him that were included in the Mitchell Report. He said that I probably did some errands for him and that I bought rims for his car. That wasn't even a good excuse, because there was no reason I would buy rims for Viña in New York and have to ship them to Milwaukee, where he played, or California, where he lived—since quality rims were available in both places.

But if telling these stories made him feel better, then I guess he felt better, but I think if he had told the truth he probably would have felt a lot better.

When Jerry Hairston Jr. claimed that he had never taken any kind of substances, it also came as a surprise to me. After the media revealed that Hairston had gotten a prescription for growth from one of those online doctors who wrote thousands of them for patients she never even met, he issued a statement saying, "It's disturbing . . . I have no idea what this is about. I'm really in the dark. Not one time have I taken steroids or anything like that. I would never do anything like that to jeopardize my career."

But I knew better. I'd met him through Segui when they were both with Baltimore. David called me one day and said, "My boy Jerry wants to talk to you." Apparently, Hairston had just had some kind of surgery on his ankle and wanted to get back on the field as quickly as possible. He was worried about his job and wanted to play; who could possibly blame him for that? I spoke with him about three different times, and during those conversations I went over everything with him, from how to store it to how to use it to what to expect. Then after he received it, he called me again and we went over everything one more time. Hairston sent me a check, but he was short of money and told me he'd catch me next time. I never heard from him again.

When my name was made public, Hairston, like a lot of other players, must have gotten real nervous, so he called David Segui to ask what he should do. David advised him, "Don't deny you know him if they ever ask. I'm telling you right now they have his checks."

"What does that mean?"

"You gave him a check. They have it." When the Mitchell Report came out, Segui was smart enough to do what every player should have done: he ducked his head and waited for it to pass over. The players who accepted reality and learned how to say "no comment" haven't really suffered. Even Jason Giambi basically won back the respect of fans by standing up and admitting that he used steroids, apologizing for it, and then going out and playing hard sober.

But the two men who denied it most vehemently—Barry Bonds and Roger Clemens—have clearly suffered the most from their lies. Bonds and Clemens should be a lesson for every ballplayer. Bonds is involved in a number of legal actions, his reputation is decimated, his chances of getting into the Hall of Fame for a long time, if ever, are pretty slim, and even though he wanted to play again in 2008, no team would risk signing him because just having him in the ballpark would have been a huge distraction. Barry Bonds was a great player long before he used any substances; if he'd admitted what he'd done that storm cloud eventually would have passed over him, as it did with Giambi, and he'd probably still be playing. But instead he claimed he had been using a nutritional supplement, flaxseed oil, and then some rubbing balm for his arthritis. While Bonds did admit getting both gel and cream steroids from BALCO, he claimed he didn't know they were illegal. Maybe if he had admitted that he used steroids he might not have regained his entire reputation, but at least people would have appreciated his achievements rather than disliking him so much for his arrogant refusal to admit what all the evidence indicates is true.

The fact that players lied or made up crazy excuses to cover up their substance use didn't surprise me at all. I think they're really surprised that they're being publicly criticized for doing the same thing so many other players were doing. But I'm also pretty positive that some of them are still doing it.

Still, even after everything I've learned and witnessed, I don't hold the players or myself entirely to blame for the steroids scandal. I'm not even that shocked that some players felt the need to lie or invent excuses to deny their use of steroids. The years I spent in the clubhouse taught me that major-league players live in a universe that revolves around them, and usually players can get away with almost anything they say and do. I think that at the time the Mitchell Report came out, a lot of the players were surprised that the public cared about steroid use as much as it did. Baseball, as an industry, looked the other way for years when baseball players like Mark McGwire, Sammy Sosa, Barry Bonds, and many others were juicing. It didn't enforce or change its own rules until the government investigated. The players named in the Mitchell Report were scrutinized, but that just scratched the surface. If the public wants to hold an entity accountable, it should take a careful look at the commissioner's office, the Players Association, and the front offices of every club across the country.

ELEVEN

In 1970 Pirates pitcher Dock Ellis threw a no-hitter against the San Diego Padres. Years later Ellis admitted that during the game he was tripping on LSD: "The ball was small sometimes, the ball was large sometimes, on one pitch I saw the catcher, while on the next I didn't. Occasionally I tried to stare the hitter down and throw while I was looking at him. I chewed my gum until it turned to powder. Other people told me I had about three or four fielding chances. I remember diving out of the way of a ball I thought was a line drive. I jumped into the air, but the ball wasn't hit hard and never reached me."

Three years after Ellis's admission, Commissioner Bowie Kuhn said that because of baseball's education and prevention efforts the sport had "no significant problem" with drugs.

At least Ellis admitted the truth. Baseball has always had problems with substance abuse; it's just that the substances have changed over the years, from Babe Ruth's well-publicized drinking to the current use of designer performance-enhancing drugs. The one thing that has been consistent throughout history is that baseball's drug policies have been inconsistent, arbitrary, and often irrational. Anabolic steroids and growth are just the latest substances players are using to try to get an edge, and they are far from the most dangerous. Any drug available to the general population has been used and abused by professional athletes, including baseball players—but major-league baseball has always done a great job of hiding it from fans.

Almost everything a player puts in his body affects his performance. Legal substances can have almost as much effect as illegal ones. For instance, caffeine is a natural stimulant. When I was with the Mets, we would go through twenty pots of coffee during a game. Players would come in every inning and chug a cup of black coffee to get an instant rush of energy. Fortunately, we had a bathroom right down the stairs from the dugout and between innings guys would rush for it. It could be pretty funny, because at times there'd be players out in the field getting desperate for the third out to be made because that coffee was running right through their system.

Tobacco and alcohol definitely affect a player's performance, but it was perfectly acceptable to abuse them when I worked in baseball. Alcohol certainly affects a player's performance, but Babe Ruth's drinking wasn't condemned—it instead became a big part of his legend. Until recently, chewing tobacco was common in the dugouts and other players actually smoked cigarettes there. I remember that when Mets pitcher Pete Harnisch finally stopped dipping, which is what we called using chew, he had terrible withdrawal problems. He couldn't sleep, got depressed, and finally had to take a leave of absence. And that was just withdrawal from tobacco, which is nothing compared to the recreational drugs some players did.

I remember attending a party with a bunch of Mets players and their wives and agents in the late 1980s. Throughout the entire party, different people kept going upstairs and into a large bathroom. When I went up there, I saw three players walking out. When I walked inside, I saw lines of cocaine laid out on a counter. I turned around and walked out. I didn't touch it. I have no doubt that the front office knew what was going on. On just about every major-league team there is at least one player who tells the executives upstairs what's going on in the clubhouse or with the team outside the stadium; he's the informer. In the clubhouse he's known as the "pipeline."

While I was with the Mets, everyone knew who the pipeline was during any given season. When he walked around, players would actually say, "Watch out, the pipeline's coming." For a while, it was a high-profile pitcher. I don't have any doubt that the pipeline told the front office about other players using cocaine, but rather than taking legal or public action, the front office handled everything in house. The Mets had a substance abuse counselor on hand just for that purpose—there were no penalties, no publicity.

But more than any other performance-enhancing substance, amphetamines had been an accepted part of the game since decades before I got involved. Long before the so-called steroid era, there was the amphetamine era or, probably more accurately, the amphetamine decades. As far back as 1969, Jim Bouton wrote in his book *Ball Four* that players were using "uppers" or "beans." Amphetamines definitely are performance-enhancing drugs and can be much more powerful than steroids. I believe uppers had a much greater impact on the game, for a lot longer period of time, than either steroids or growth hormones.

What amphetamines do is raise your adrenaline level, make your heart pump faster, and make you stronger right away. The physical response is almost instantaneous. Players liked using them because they allowed them to zone in. Players got so focused on the moment that they weren't even aware that fifty thousand people were screaming at them. The biggest difference between amphetamines and steroids is that the effect of amphetamines lasts for a much shorter time than even really mild steroids.

When I was in the clubhouse, baseball players took uppers like candy. Comparing the number of players who used amphetamines to the number of players who used steroids is like comparing apples to diamonds. If there were 1,000 players in the league, 990 took uppers. I know that Pete Rose was using them because his son, Pete Rose Jr., told me once, "My father would never play without using them."

Players didn't take them for every game, only when they needed that extra energy boost. I always knew who had taken them because after the game they'd be drinking milk. Players drank milk because the lactose and calcium helped their body digest the amphetamine, which meant they came off the high much faster.

Amphetamines are inexpensive, easily available, very effective, and an accepted part of the game. Players would "bean up." Everybody knew they were sort of vaguely illegal, but they were so common in baseball that nobody was concerned about getting caught. It was an open secret: nobody talked about it out loud, and reporters never wrote a word about it.

David Segui played while amphetamines were rampant, and he told me, "A lot of guys lied about it. I don't know why; it wasn't considered a terrible thing to be doing. But I had people going into my locker trying to find what I had. The clubhouse guys told me. I'd bring a couple with me and hide them in my pants pockets. I had to do that or the players who didn't want anyone to know they were taking beans would clean me out."

The 162-game schedule takes an incredible toll on players. With all the traveling involved, with day games after night games, nobody ever gets enough sleep. It's an incredible grind. Amphetamines were one of the substances that allowed players to play 150 games each season; they helped them to be up for a day game after the previous night's game had ended only a few hours earlier. In those situations, amphetamines will make a difference—but anabolics or HGH won't.

I tried uppers once or twice when I was in high school. While I was working for the Mets, I had to study for the SATs. I was exhausted and I thought I needed the kick to stay up late to study. As it turned out, the high was way too strong for me. It definitely kept me awake, but it also made me incredibly jittery. So I never did it again.

Personally, I think amphetamines are potentially much more dangerous than steroids, because uppers affect your heart and can be deadly if a person has undiagnosed medical problems. I had a lot of guys ask me about the drug's safety, and I always replied, "I don't think it's a good idea. That's messing with your body chemistry and you just don't want to do that."

But a lot of players chose to use uppers anyway, and the drug was really easy to obtain. Like steroids, amphetamines are sold at most gyms and even over the counter in pharmacies in South America.

Hispanic players would bring uppers back from home at the beginning of the season, or their families would bring a bag when they came for a visit. Americans who played winter ball would load up on their supply for the season, since most players knew exactly how many pills they needed. When we played in San Diego, there would be a line of players walking across the border to Tijuana. Not to mention that, now, uppers are available all over the Internet.

Amphetamines are available in a million different forms. They're in diet pills like fen-phen, narcolepsy medicine, and every attention deficit disorder medicine, including Ritalin. In fact as soon as players figured out what was in prescription medicines for ADD, two hundred players suddenly realized that they were undiagnosed.

Also, just like steroids, to get any real benefit from uppers it helped if a player knew what he was doing. There are a hundred different types, and some are better suited for certain conditions. There's one that's better to use if it's hot; another one is preferable when it's cold. Amphetamines are time released, and with some kinds the effects only last about an hour, which meant that sometimes players actually had to take a second pill in the middle of a game. The pills come in every color, but undoubtedly the best known are the "greenies," which come out of your system rapidly: a fifth-inning pill for ballplayers.

The line between legal and illegal substances can be very blurry. Amphetamines are illegal, for example, but for the most part dietary supplements are legal and barely regulated. Supplements provide the protein you need in order to build muscle, but what makes them different from steroids is that they build up a body over a longer period of time and generally don't produce dramatic results.

If you just drank protein shakes and exercised, you'd build muscle. By the time I quit the Mets, most of the players were using at least one supplement on a regular basis, mostly a common product like MET-Rx. Supplements come in various forms, from powders to energy drinks, and they generally contain some combination of vitamins, minerals, herbs and other botanicals, amino acids, and whatever else the manufacture decides to put into them. It's common to have as many as thirty different vitamins in one supplement. The laws governing the use of supplements are pretty vague because the government treats supplements as food rather than a drug. In 1994 Congress passed the Dietary Supplement Health and Education Act, but all that did was force the FDA to prove that a specific supplement was dangerous before it could ban its sale.

The reality is that supplements are a multibillion-dollar, loosely regulated industry that pretty much does anything it wants to do. Some companies produce excellent products, but there are a lot of shady companies that sell garbage. Ironically, it was a supplement that started the steroids scandal in baseball and eventually led the government to me.

This whole scandal really began one night in July 1998, during the celebrated home run race between Mark McGwire and Sammy Sosa. An Associated Press features writer named Steve Wilstein was waiting by McGwire's locker for him to appear for an interview after a game. While Wilstein waited, he began writing down everything he saw in the locker. There was a cap from a Roger Maris golf tournament, pictures of McGwire's son, and a brown bottle labeled "androstenedione."

Wilstein didn't have the slightest idea what andro was until he checked with a doctor, and then he realized he had a big story. The doctor told Wilstein that andro was a completely legal, over-the-counter supplement—but after it was ingested, the body rapidly converted it into an illegal anabolic steroid. It was legal to sell, legal to take, but illegal once it dissolved in McGwire's body—at least if he was playing in the NFL, the NCAA, or the Olympics, which had already banned its use. But under baseball's drug policy it was perfectly acceptable. Everybody in the gym knew all about andro; while it built muscle, andro also could damage the liver and reproductive organs.

When Wilstein's story came out, the Cardinals denied that McGwire was taking it, but eventually McGwire himself admitted it. "Everything I've done is natural," he said. "Everybody I know in the game of baseball uses the same stuff I use." Baseball didn't care since the home run race between McGwire and Sosa was bringing fans back into the ballpark. Commissioner Bud Selig responded by ignoring it; instead telling reporters, "I think what Mark McGwire has accomplished is so remarkable, and he has handled it so beautifully, we want to do everything we can to enjoy a great moment in baseball history."

I was pleased when I read the stories about McGwire. The fact that Selig wanted the press to ignore andro was actually reassuring to me, since I had just started supplying steroids to players. To me the difference between andro—and other supplements that converted to anabolics, like creatine—and actual steroids was awfully slim. At the time I probably figured that if baseball wasn't going to do anything about supplements, it definitely wasn't going to make a big deal about the real product.

When both baseball and the government banned the sale of andro, players began using another legal supplement, creatine, which had pretty much the same effect. When kids read that their heroes were using these legal supplements they began buying the same products. McGwire wasn't just a role model—he turned out to be a slugging advertisement for the whole industry.

I'm knowledgeable about supplements, but I'm not an expert. There are just too many companies selling too many different products for me to know everything. Companies mix and match supplements frequently. I try to keep up, but it's almost impossible to know about everything on the market. When people asked me to recommend a product, I would tell them to buy supplements made by certain companies that I knew from experience sold reliable products.

The perception is that the use of steroids and human growth hormones is being treated more seriously by baseball than the other substances players have used in the past. As far as my life is concerned, that's true: I'm a convicted felon because for the first time the government got involved. But the players who used them haven't been penalized like other major leaguers have been for using recreational drugs—except in public opinion.

In the past, major-league baseball had tried to avoid enforcing a serious drug policy, but that changed when the cocaine epidemic hit America in the 1980s and '90s. For example, pitcher Steve Howe was suspended seven different times during his seventeen-year career for cocaine and alcohol abuse, or as he once said, "I was the first to be fried and tried." But even after he was supposedly suspended for life, he was reinstated.

Doc Gooden, my friend, just couldn't beat his addiction, and after testing positive for cocaine once too often, he was suspended for the entire 1996 season. Hall of Fame pitcher Ferguson Jenkins was caught trying to cross the Canadian border with cocaine, hashish, and marijuana, and, besides a brief suspension, the biggest penalty he received was that it took him eight years after he retired to be voted into the Hall of Fame. But even after baseball instituted tougher penalties for using banned substances, players were convinced they could still get away with using whatever they wanted to use.

The general feeling in the clubhouse about steroids and amphetamines when I worked for the Mets was that baseball wanted a program that looked from the outside like it was effective, but didn't want to enforce it from within. New stadiums were being built, attendance was booming, revenue was up, so the owners didn't want to do anything at all to affect baseball's popularity. But because of all the negative publicity, the public had to believe that baseball was taking action.

The Players Association has continually fought baseball's efforts to institute a drug-testing program. Not that baseball ever really tried very hard. Beginning in 1971, baseball prohibited the nonprescription use, possession, or distribution of drugs. That was the confused policy in place when players like Howe, Jenkins, and Gooden were suspended.

The reality, as I've mentioned, is that baseball has always tolerated cheating; it's as much a part of the game as peanuts, popcorn, and amphetamines. Until the commissioner's office was forced to put on its big phony show of surprise and horror when all of this became public, baseball had long tolerated the use of performance-enhancing substances. It just looked the other way, and to a certain extent it had no choice. The Players Association took every legal step possible to prevent the commissioner from instituting or enforcing tougher rules on players.

I don't care what claims other people make, everybody in baseball knew what was going on—but the last thing they wanted to do was talk about it. The executives, the players, the coaches, the trainers, they all knew and ignored it. Coaches get paid to be aware of the small things. Are they not going to notice a substantial change in a player's build? Trainers work with players every day: suddenly a player gains substantial muscle in a few weeks and they're going to believe it all came from working out? Sammy Sosa's weight fluctuated between 165 pounds and 230! Everybody noticed, from the sportswriters, who didn't write about it because they needed to maintain the cooperation of the players to do their job, to the agents, who sometimes pushed their clients to do it.

Agents are often in a position to know more about what's going on in professional sports than club executives and player's wives. Occasionally, when a player mailed me a payment, the return address would be an agency. When Kevin Brown sent me thousands of dollars in cash, in twenty-dollar bills, by FedEx, the package had his agent's return address on it. If any player's agent knew his client was using the agent's address to send large amounts of cash like that, don't you think the agent might have asked why he was sending someone $10,000 in small bills rather than a check? This was baseball, not *CSI*.

I know for a fact that some agents pushed their players to talk to me. They would ask another one of their clients to make the introduction. It made sense for agents to do that because the better their clients did, the bigger contracts they could negotiate, and the higher commission they would earn. Many of these agents are lawyers, so they knew the legal ramifications, but they also knew how to skirt the truth better than their clients and weren't going to admit anything. I knew several of the agents, which was surprising because apparently none of them knew me. I remember one agent who forgot he knew me telling me at a Christmas party, "I want to thank you for helping my guy out. You're doing a great job." Another agent thanked me for putting his client on a program, because, "He's knocking the shit out of it."

Anyone who was around baseball at that time and claims they didn't know what was going on is either lying or one of the dumbest people on the planet. The owners knew too. Before investing tens of millions of dollars in a long-term contract, don't you think an owner would do enough research to find out if the player is using a performance-enhancing substance? Two decades ago, I know for a fact that the Mets knew what most players were doing at night, including Doc and Straw. Management hired people to follow them, so the front office knew what clubs their players went to, who their stars were there with—and why not? If clubs were compiling that information that long ago, I'd have to believe teams continued to do it before offering a player multimillion-dollar contracts.

There's no doubt in my mind that when George W. Bush was an owner of the Texas Rangers he must have known what was going on. There were some great players on that Rangers team, and several of them have either been accused of or have admitted to using, among them Rafael Palmeiro, David Segui, and Iván Rodríguez. Personally, I don't think it's possible for that many stars on a team to be using without ownership knowing about it. So unless George Bush was not playing an active role in that ownership situation, he had to know.

But nobody really felt it was necessary to do anything about it until Barry Bonds attracted so much attention to the problem when he hit seventy-three home runs in 2001. He got too good, combined with the fact that a lot of baseball people just despised him because he was so arrogant. So people started chirping a little. Bonds led to BALCO, which led eventually to Giambi and Clemens and, unfortunately, Radomski. Baseball was forced to take action it probably would never have taken.

Baseball's drug policy officially began changing in 2002. By that time organized baseball had already instituted a much more extensive drug-testing policy in the minor leagues—players not on a major-league roster could be tested twice during and after the season for a variety of drugs, including steroids, amphetamines, and marijuana, and could be suspended for as long as a season if they tested positive four times. But even as late as the 2008 season, minor-league teams admitted that they were getting at least a day's notice before the drug tester showed up—enough time for players to take steps to get rid of some of the substances in their system.

Major leaguers, though, were pretty much protected by the Players Association from being randomly tested. But in 2002 the basic agreement between baseball and the union changed. For the first time, players on a major-league club's forty-man roster were prohibited from using anabolic steroids, and mandatory random drug testing was permitted. While that policy sounded tough on paper, it actually wasn't that effective in reality because the union had the right to challenge any disciplinary action taken by baseball for violations of the drug policy. In other words, the 2002 policy had a lot of gums to it, but no teeth. Even the limited testing for performance-enhancing drugs covered by the agreement was restricted only to steroids; it didn't include amphetamines—which at that point future Hall of Famer Tony Gwynn estimated as many as half of all major leaguers were using—or supplements like andro and creatine.

Also in that 2002 agreement, baseball and the union agreed that all twelve hundred major-league players would be anonymously tested for steroids—half of them during spring training—and if more than 5 percent tested positive then baseball could begin a random testing program, which would include penalties for testing positive. I think that baseball was actually counting on the fact that players would be smart enough to avoid testing positive. It shouldn't have been too difficult since most steroids that players used left their bodies within a few weeks. If a player stopped taking substances a couple of weeks before the beginning of spring training, he would test negative and couldn't be tested again that season, which was basically an intentional pass. The purpose of the anonymous testing supposedly was to determine the extent of the problem but not to find out which players were juicing—or to punish individuals.

I got a lot of calls from players who wanted to talk about how to tailor their use of the banned substances to make sure they tested negative. Nobody was worried about their career since there were no penalties, but a lot of my guys were concerned about their public image. I couldn't piss for everybody, so I told them what to do. "You have to use a water-based steroid," I explained. So the few clients I had who were still taking steroids limited their use to water-based products that quickly left their system. The players using growth had nothing to worry about because there isn't a test available that can detect it.

The story I heard—and I have absolutely no idea if it's true—is that baseball did everything possible to make sure that less than 5 percent of the players tested positive. Supposedly, the tests weren't random—baseball intentionally stayed away from players rumored to be juicing to keep the numbers down. Instead younger players and journeymen players were tested. But what baseball hadn't anticipated was the extent of steroid use in Caribbean winter baseball leagues. I had players tell me that they had trainers there who would give them injections of anything they wanted. The players had to buy the stuff at a pharmacy, bring it to the clubhouse, and the trainer would actually inject them. A lot of people who had played winter ball weren't even aware that the testing program would begin in spring training, and as a result a large number tested positive.

It also turned out that the anonymous testing wasn't anonymous at all. Each player was given a code number that matched his name—so anyone with access to the code list would know which players tested positive. When the grand jury began investigating BALCO, it received a copy of that list. It turned out that ninety players had tested positive. Apparently the Players Association informed those players of the outcome of their tests. As Senator Mitchell reported, "A former major league player stated in 2003 he was tested as part of the survey testing program. He said that in September 2004, Gene Orza of the Players Association told him he had tested positive in 2003 and that he would be tested in the next weeks."

I knew that Senator Mitchell was quoting David Segui, because David had told me exactly the same thing. He said he was approached by baseball executives who had warned him that he was going to be tested within the next two weeks. David also said that other big-name players were also notified in the same way.

Another one of my clients told me how he found out the results of his test: "When a team would come to New York, someone from the commissioner's office would ask the players who failed to come into the city for a meeting. I didn't want to go, so I kept asking the person who called me what the meeting was all about. Finally, he told me, 'Well, we want to let you know you tested positive.'

"I told them, 'Wait a second, I thought this was supposed to be anonymous?' They had no answer for that one."

Both Jason Grimsley and Larry Bigbie also said that they'd been told that they had failed the obviously not-so-anonymous tests in 2003.

After the 5-percent-positive threshold was passed, baseball had an even bigger problem: it had to officially institute random testing with penalties. Every player could be tested once during the season and then once in the off-season. The first time a player tested positive he was suspended for ten days; the fourth time he was suspended for a year without pay. Growth hormones were also added to the list of prohibited substances, although the only test for them was urine analysis, which is worthless because growth hormones don't show up in urine. While these penalties seemed severe, base-ball still did not include amphetamines or supplements like cre-atine on the list of banned substances. But even when the tougher rules went into effect, not one single player called me in a state of panic. Instead they'd ask me, "What do I have to stay away from? What can I do?"

I got all the information I needed about how long each steroid stays in the body and I kept it near the phone. When they asked I'd lay it out for them: "Take this one. It takes four weeks. Deca stays eighteen months so it's out of the question. No more Deca," I told them. "That's over." Surprisingly, the new drug policy wasn't a big deal.

I was still pretty sure that baseball didn't actually want to catch players. I was told that when punitive testing of players began in 2004, some players were informed when they were going to be tested. I don't have any specific evidence of that, it's just the rumors that I heard, but the logic is impossible to ignore: the absolute last thing an owner wants is to have the star player he's paying six mil-lion dollars to be suspended. Nobody talks about it, but the truth is that fans don't care what a player is doing privately as long as he's performing on the field; they just want their team to win. Baseball doesn't care, since as an industry, it's drawing more customers and making more money than ever before in history. The Players Asso-ciation doesn't care, since its job is to protect major-league players; and if possible, I believe it would end all testing.

Whatever happened, early in 2005 Commissioner Selig an-nounced that he was "startled" by the fact that in almost twelve hundred tests conducted in the second half of the 2004 season, the percentage of players who tested positive for steroids dropped to between 1 percent and 2 percent. "With our new program," he said, "I am very confident that we will have effectively rid our sport of steroids in this coming season." Of course, the commissioner neglected to mention that for whatever reasons baseball had very quietly suspended testing for a time during 2004, a fact he also neglected to mention a year later when he testified in front of Congress. When it came out later, Selig had to write an explanatory letter to Congress, telling them why he had forgotten to mention that little detail. It's possible Selig believed that testing was effective. After all, there are still people who believe that the United States never landed on the moon.

Any chance that this wasn't going to become a big scandal that led directly to me ended when José Canseco's book *Juiced* was published in 2005. Everybody was talking about the book, wondering how they were going to be affected. Several players who knew Canseco told me that he was angry at baseball because he believed that the league had blackballed him so that he wouldn't reach 500 home runs. At the time, Canseco had hit 462 home runs in his career and knew that membership in baseball's 500-home-run club would be worth a fortune at autograph and memorabilia shows.

I was also told by people I considered knowledgeable that Canseco had approached players and asked them to pay him not to be mentioned in *Juiced* and then its sequel, *Vindicated*. Someone very close to Roger Clemens told me before *Juiced* was published that Clemens had paid Canseco twenty-five thousand dollars not to be mentioned, and an additional sum, probably fifty thousand dollars, for Canseco to write that Roger didn't cheat on his wife. Although

I have no proof that any of that is true, I trusted the person who told me that, and when the book came out, it happened to mention that Clemens had never cheated on his wife. It was a question that no one had asked Canseco to write about, and an odd factoid given that Canseco and Clemens had never even played together.

When Canseco was working on the sequel to his book, Magglio Ordóñez told reporters that Canseco had asked him to invest five million dollars in the documentary he supposedly was making about steroid use in return for not being named in the second book.

What Canseco really did was force baseball to take more action. After BALCO, baseball had successfully made Bonds out to be a scapegoat, and because Bonds wasn't popular, it looked like that effort might be successful. But after *Juiced* was published, there was just too much publicity for baseball to ignore steroid use any longer. Congress also did nothing about it, but at least it appeared that the government had taken action.

Because of the negative publicity, at the end of the 2005 season baseball and the Players Association agreed to institute an even tougher punitive drug program: players would be suspended for fifty games if they tested positive once, one hundred games for the second positive result, and banned for life after a third positive test. Those are serious penalties that could cost a player millions of dollars, but truthfully there was no change in the number of phone calls I received. The main difference was that more players wanted growth hormones, knowing that they were undetectable in drug tests.

What players were more worried about than beating the test

was how to hide the physical effects of the juice from the public. Nobody wanted to blow up like Bonds—and Dykstra years before him—which would attract attention to them and start gossip. In that respect, I was really valuable to my clients because I worked with them and designed individual programs that minimized any obvious physical changes. I gave the players I worked with a complete plan for the entire length of time they were taking the stuff. They would do a pyramid, starting with a small dosage and working their way up, then reducing the dosage. There were also over-the-counter products that players could take to counteract the steroids. So players would gain what they needed, but any physical change was gradual and, equally as important, my clients didn't crash when they came off it. Everything had to be done according to a plan. So no one would be able to notice a muscle gain or see a change in personality. Everything was smooth.

The only thing testing has done is give baseball cover, making it look like it is actually accomplishing something. But testing doesn't work. It's a serious joke. There are too many ways to beat the tests, and too much money involved, not to do it. Since baseball began testing quite a few minor-league players have tested positive and been suspended, as well as a couple of major leaguers, but these were players who either had bad advice or simply didn't know what they were doing.

I absolutely guarantee that major-league players have never stopped taking growth hormones and steroids. I guarantee it— although, and let me say this directly to Senator Mitchell, Jeff Novitzky, and Matt Parrella, I no longer have any personal knowledge of it.

The main criticism I've received from fans is that I helped cheapen the history of the game. There are probably a lot of people who believe that the substances I distributed enabled players to break baseball's cherished home run records. As has been pointed out to me several times, even Senator Mitchell wrote that the "widespread use of such substances . . . raises questions about the validity of baseball records."

I don't believe that at all. In fact anyone who believes that players have broken these records because they were using steroids or growth hormones doesn't know enough about baseball. Let me make clear one more time that the biggest impact steroids and growth hormones had was that they enabled players to perform at the peak of their ability on a regular basis and helped them to keep their stamina during the second half of the season. Those changes alone led many players to end up with better stats.

Even Bill James, who changed baseball management with his unique statistical analysis of the game, doesn't believe the increased offensive output was caused by steroids, instead explaining that it is probably due to a combination of the numerous changes that have taken place in baseball during the last decade. The game has changed totally since the day I walked into the Mets clubhouse. It was during that time that baseball stopped being a sport and became a big business. The players, the equipment they use, the routines they follow in and out of the season, even the stadiums have very little resemblance to the way the major leagues operated just two decades ago. Fred Wilpon wasn't the only owner who stopped giving away broken bats. With the potential for huge profits, owners began investing more money in their teams, hired more coaches, built video rooms, brought in all types of specialists, and did anything else possible to increase run production and to make the game more entertaining for the fans—all of which worked.

Real fans know that the game changes substantially about every generation. For example, before the 1970s managers didn't rely on relief pitchers, so in the late innings of a game hitters like Willie Mays and Mickey Mantle were facing pitchers who had already thrown 110 pitches or more. It's pretty obvious that a batter has a better shot when he's facing an exhausted pitcher rather than a fresh relief pitcher.

Baseball also added more offense by getting umpires to reduce the strike zone, forcing pitchers to throw more pitches in hittable areas. In addition baseball expanded from twenty-six to thirty teams, including in Denver, where the combination of high altitude and thin air meant balls were going to go flying out of Coors Field, diluting the quality of what was already watered-down pitching.

I believe the multimillion-dollar contracts had as much to do with the increased production as did the use of any substance. Until the late 1980s, for most major-league players baseball was a part-time job; it was the big salaries that allowed it to become a full-time profession. Two decades ago players had to work during the off-season to meet their expenses. Each spring I'd see the players straggle into camp overweight and out of shape. There were only a handful of guys who trained. The multimillion-dollar annual salaries these guys are now earning not only made it possible, they made it absolutely necessary, for major leaguers to concentrate on baseball throughout the whole year.

While most minor leaguers still have to earn a living during the winter, major leaguers work out with personal trainers, often in their own home gyms, and they follow programs tailored to their needs by nutritionists and dieticians. As a result they are never out of shape. Even those players who have never used the juice in their lives take supplements and other health-related substances. I created off-season programs for a lot of players. Generally, those programs included creatine, which builds muscle, and a daily multivitamin. I'm a big believer in vitamins, and I would often send vitamins to my clients with their other substances. I would also tell players that they absolutely had to take the supplement glucosamine to keep their joints lubricated, and sometimes I would also advise my guys to take a legal prohormone like Supradol. Everybody I worked with ate a high-protein diet as well. I guaranteed that any player who worked out regularly and followed my program was going to get bigger and stronger, and would have more stamina throughout the entire season—without using a single banned substance.

By itself a year-round program like this is going to make a substantial difference in the numbers a player puts up. The reason I was able to wake up in the clubhouse and hit two home runs in the Mets front office and media game was because I'd been working out every week for years, not because I'd stuck a needle in my body. It was a cumulative effect, not a magic potion.

The equipment that players use has also been greatly improved. Players today use bats with larger barrels and thinner handles than ever before, which allows them to whip them through the strike zone with greater force. A lot of those bats are now made of maple, which seems to shatter more easily than traditional bats made from ash, and accounts for the increased number of broken bats. Faster bat speed and the added weight in the barrel equal increased power. Even the use of pine tar and batting gloves allows players to grip the bat more tightly to increase bat speed. Also, most players tell me that baseballs differ. The more tightly wound a ball, the farther it's going to go. The lower the laces, the more difficult it is for pitchers to throw breaking pitches. In 2006, for example, after the new ban on steroids was put in place, Orioles pitching coach Leo Mazzone admitted, "I swear a lot of balls look like Titleists hit with a two iron—only they're flying a lot farther."

Among the new types of equipment players are using are arm braces, which offer real protection when they lean out over the plate. Batters aren't afraid of getting hit. A consultant for the St. Louis Cardinals who researched the effect of Barry Bonds's arm brace refers to it as a hitting machine. It actually has moveable parts that lock Bonds's elbow into a level hitting position. Padres general manager Kevin Towers said that because of those protective pads, "Pitchers don't pitch inside as much . . . I can understand [using a brace] if you're coming off an injury, but not for an entire career. Look at Bonds and what he's wearing. That's a joke."

Added to all the other evidence is the fact that there have been almost two dozen new stadiums built around the country in the last two decades, and in just about every one of them the dimensions have been reduced. They call these new ballparks in cities like Houston and Baltimore "retro" or "cozy," but the fences were brought in to produce more home runs.

The records are being broken because more home runs are being hit now than ever before. Why more home runs are being hit: players are bigger and stronger and they're hitting with harder bats in smaller ballparks off mediocre pitching. Of course there has been an increase in home run stats—for everyone.

Personally, I think it's pretty obvious that contrary to all the complaints, steroids and growth hormones have not ruined the game. If anything, I believe they helped save it after the players' strike. The biggest records that were broken in the so-called steroids era were the attendance records. In 2007 baseball set records for both total attendance and average attendance at games: twenty-three of the thirty teams had an increase in attendance and eight teams set attendance records. So it's hard to figure out exactly what terrible damage steroids have done.

I know it makes a good story, but there was never any crisis in confidence about the integrity of the game on the part of either the players or, really, the public. It's unbelievable to me that steroid use in baseball has received far more publicity than pro basketball's scandal, in which referees bet on games they worked in. Considering the potential scope of that problem, I think the NBA would be thrilled to be dealing with a steroid issue.

I know I broke the law, and I've been penalized for that. I have no complaints about the way I have been treated. But I also believe that I can say accurately that if it hadn't been me supplying these substances to major-league players they simply would have gotten them someplace else—and maybe used them in a dangerous fashion.

My friend David Segui has told people that baseball should be grateful to me for protecting its multimillion-dollar investments, for making sure that my players used substances safely. I seriously doubt I'm ever going to receive a thank-you note from major-league baseball, but the use of steroids and growth hormones by athletes isn't going to end either. Anyone who believes it's possible to eliminate these drugs from all sports by creating rules, policing the players, and punishing people who test positive probably also believes that Clemens never touched the stuff. Athletes are never going to stop looking for the edge. They're too competitive and the payoffs are too big.

We've seen how unsuccessful the so-called war on drugs has been in this country, so how does it make sense to repeat that strategy with performance-enhancing drugs? Instead of wasting time trying to eliminate them from sports or society, we should deal with reality. We should educate people about the potential dangers of steroids and HGH, particularly to young people. We should regulate and monitor their use, and support law enforcement's efforts to go after those companies that sell any of these substances to minors.

Baseball desperately wants fans to believe that the steps it has taken have effectively eliminated the use of steroids and growth hormones from the major leagues, but I don't believe it. It's impossible. I guarantee that for every athlete that who tested positive there are many more who have figured out how to beat the tests. There is almost always a scientific equivalent of me pissing in a metal cigar holder for Doc Gooden.

If baseball is serious about trying to eliminate these substances, the penalties for their use have to be severe and strictly enforced. I don't think that will work, but the current policy definitely doesn't serve as a major deterrent to players.

Realistically, though, I don't think baseball is going to try to increase penalties, because the Players Association wouldn't allow it.

Instead I think what baseball should do is take an honest look at the value of these substances and find a way to regulate their use. Growth hormones in particular can be unbelievably beneficial in getting players back on the field where they're supposed to be. Rather than making some arbitrary decision based on hysteria and perception, baseball should create a realistic policy, especially because these substances, and others that will follow, are not going to be eliminated.

But I know that won't happen either. Instead baseball will muddle along with a haphazard policy, basically waiting and hoping that fans forget about the issue. That will be exactly what happens.

EPILOGUE

I can't pick out a specific incident and say that it's when everything started. Maybe it all began when I walked into a gym and knew that I belonged there, or it could have been when Lenny Dykstra showed up in spring training all new and improved. Perhaps it was the first time I told a player, "Don't worry, I'll get it for you." But I didn't plan any part of what happened. I'm just a guy with knowledge and contacts, who was very useful, and who was involved with baseball at the right time. Or, considering the way things turned out for me, maybe I was a person who happened to be around the major leagues at the wrong time.

On the flight home from San Francisco after being sentenced, I tried to make some sense out of everything that I'd been through during the previous year. I had been leading a relatively normal, completely anonymous life until the morning Jeff Novitzky's team knocked on my door. Looking back, it seemed like only an instant had passed between that moment and when, only a few hours before, I was pushing my way through a mob of reporters and photographers, trying to get out of the courtroom after I was sentenced. For the whole year I felt like I was living in a completely foreign world.

I hated every minute of it. Not because going to prison scared me, though, because I knew I was capable of doing time if I had to. The truth was that I feared I wouldn't be able to take care of my family, the most important part of my life. While I sat on that airplane, I swore that I'd never touch an illegal substance again.

Today my life is about as normal as it can be. I get up every morning and go to work, and most of the time I'm completely out of the spotlight. I get a few phone calls from reporters every time there's a steroid story in the news, but otherwise the media leaves me alone. Nearly all my friends from baseball are gone. The only former player I still speak to is David Segui, and of course I'm still very close to trainer Brian McNamee—but both of those guys were my best friends before all this happened, and they will continue to be my friends long after.

I'm on probation for my actions and will be for the next few years, but the real punishment will outlast my life. I have no doubt that when I die my obituary will identify me as the key figure in baseball's steroid scandal. No matter what good I do for the rest of my life, even if win two Nobel Prizes—highly unlikely, I know—Kirk Radomski will always be known as baseball's steroid pusher. That's my legacy, and I guess I chose it.

I don't watch baseball too much on television and I never go to the ballpark; even when I was working for the Mets I was never really a fan. From time to time I'll sit down in my den and put on a game. If one of my former clients is playing, I'll watch for a while. Sometimes I think about the players and how their friendships were a huge part of my life for so many years. But most often, I'm too busy with today to think about the past. That part of my life is over, and I don't miss it at all.